WHOLE HEARTED

Companion Workbook

Self-leadership for women in transition

TERRI CONNELLAN

Copyright © 2021 Terri Connellan
First published by the kind press, 2021

All rights reserved. No part of this book may be reproduced, stored in a retrieval system or transmitted in any form or by any means, electronic, mechanical photocopying, recording, or otherwise, without written permission from the author and publisher.

This publication contains the opinions and ideas of its author. It is intended to provide helpful and informative material on the subjects addressed in the publication. While the publisher and author have used their best efforts in preparing this book, the material in this book is of the nature of general comment only. It is sold with the understanding that the author and publisher are not engaged in rendering advice or any other kind of personal professional service in the book. In the event that you use any of the information in this book for yourself, the author and the publisher assume no responsibility for your actions.

Cover and internal design by Nada Backovic
Edited by Dr Juliet Richters
Cover images by iStock
Logo by Stephey Baker of Marked by the Muse

NATIONAL LIBRARY OF AUSTRALIA Cataloguing-in-Publication entry is available from the National Library Australia.

ISBN 978-0-6451392-0-4
ISBN 978-0-6450887-9-3 (ebook)

FOREWORD

Once upon a time, a well-respected government organisation looked after its employees and cared about them; it supported them and wanted the best for them. For a young woman wanting to make a difference and to blend her love of writing and teaching into a profession, it offered the perfect place to commence crafting a professional life. While she didn't start out intending to spend thirty years of her life working there, that's exactly what happened.

The organisation was interested in its workers and valued their skills, knowledge and experience and then one day, with a change of leadership, that heart was lost. This wholehearted girl had trouble believing anymore in the promises of the organisation, which spluttered under the stress of restructuring to become leaner and more commercial. Each time she tried to apply for jobs within the organisation, even while she continued to provide essential support to its key leaders through the transition at hand, she kept getting rebuffed. It confused her. Was her heart not in it anymore, or was it the organisation that had moved on and left her behind?

It would have been so easy in these circumstances to leave herself behind. To leave pieces of her heart on the altar of the organisation, like sacrifices. But enough was enough—a heart given over thirty years day in, day out is enough.

And so she turned to rediscover what she really felt wholehearted about. What turned her on? What lit up her soul before the government got in the way and stole all those precious years, like a thoughtless thief?

Settled in a quiet place of inspiration, she made a plan. It started with a list of her passions and learnings. As she scribbled down everything she had learnt in the process of her job and her life, she saw patterns. It kept circling back to a few core interests and qualities in the end: reading, books, writing, poetry, personality type, introversion, intuition, creativity, leadership, innovation, flowing, being connected with special others.

She returned to these essential elements so she could rediscover the lifeblood of wholeheartedness that she had lost. She read, she studied, she revisited the key books that she cherished, the music that she loved.

She went back to swimming, to walks, to nature, to yoga. And she learnt too about personality, the moon, tarot and oracle, guideposts to help with understanding the spirit and symbols that spoke to her intuitive heart.

Then, her mother got really sick. She also found out she too was unwell, burnt out from all the engagement, people, battles without a purpose, and related futile efforts to help the organisation that she loved thrive in a new environment.

But soon it took off without her, leaving her adrift, half-hearted, soul-destroyed—so Six of Swords, so Eight of Cups.

Today she is healing, still finding that transition, that path to wholeheartedness, and she is helping others along the way too. But rather than focusing her skills, knowledge, learning and efforts in support of an organisation, she directs them towards her true self and the inner life in the practice and teaching of *self-leadership*. Her days are devoted to understanding the pieces, to knowing the parts, to reclaiming the pieces taken over by the outside world and lost in the traffic of the commute, the fairytale promises of the politics, and the allure of being liked.

It is all so transparently gone now. She resides with clarity in a new space and time, as if on another planet, in a constellation of herself and others dedicated to wholehearted living—with a sun shining, planets and moons spinning, and everybody smiling, finding and sharing ways to sustain life creatively in a new paradigm.

It's no secret that the woman in the story is yours truly—and the book *Wholehearted* and this *Wholehearted Companion Workbook* my invitation to you. Come with me on the journey of how this tale unfolded. I share my learning about sacred pathways towards being more creative and wholehearted, with self-leadership as a guide. My intention is to inspire your journey through sharing my strategies, process and tips. While your journey will look different, as we are all unique, I hope that my learning and experiences might help you too.

Tips for using the Wholehearted Companion Workbook

On the way through *Wholehearted*, you will have come across questions which might act as reflection or journal prompts. This *Wholehearted Companion Workbook* provides an opportunity for a deeper dive into personal self-leadership and transition strategies to inspire your wholehearted life.

The *Wholehearted Companion Workbook* is practical, with questions you can reflect on and answer, checklists to help you prioritise personal actions and the opportunity to see more practical examples of what I have shared in *Wholehearted* from my life and learning experiences to inspire yours. The chapters and sections align with the book so you can choose how you work with it but easily cross-reference between them. Some people like to read the whole book through first then deal with the detail. Others like to apply as they go through. You choose the best way for you!

Reading *Wholehearted* and working through this *Wholehearted Companion Workbook* is a self-leadership journey in itself and I congratulate you on choosing to take the time to put yourself first and work through it. I hope this *Wholehearted Companion Workbook* inspires wholehearted self-leadership in your life so you can truly shine in your own brilliant way in the world!

CONTENTS

PART ONE   1
MY WHOLEHEARTED TRANSITION JOURNEY

1. Beginning the journey   3
1.1 Journey beginning   3
1.2 In the heart of transition   5
1.3 Transition and Turning Points   9
1.4 Self-leadership: keys to wholeness and change   11

2. Imagining another way   13
2.1 Stepping stones and lighthouses of initial inspiration and learning   13
2.2 The long haul: showing up and being brave   15
2.3 Hard inner work, not luck   24
2.4 How our self-talk guides and shapes us as we imagine a new way   25

3. Identifying your passions and what you love   29
3.1 Why identify your passions?   29
3.2 Qualities of passions   30
3.3 Finding your authentic heart   35
3.4 The unique voice of what you love: your onlyness   40

4. Identifying your natural gifts, style and desires   43
4.1 The examined life   43
4.2 Personality type and preferences   45
4.3 Understanding our preferences and gifts   47
4.4 Quiet, quiet leadership and our personal brand of strength   50
4.5 Your unique style, Style Statement and Style Type   52
4.6 Your Core Desired Feelings: how you want to feel   54

5. Identifying your body of work and resources built over time   57
5.1 Your body of work over time   57
5.2 Body of work and what it can tell us   59

5.3	Not leaving pieces of yourself behind	61
5.4	Turning points and leaving with grace	62
5.5	Resources for a new life	65
5.6	Finishing on a high note: closure, letting go and moving on	68
5.7	Job-seeking, promotions, creative opportunities	71
5.8	Reframing redundancy, being 'deleted' and obsolescence	72
5.9	Investing in our wisdom, crafting our journey and building our cathedral	74

PART TWO — 77
WHOLEHEARTED SELF-LEADERSHIP SKILLS

6. Wholehearted self-leadership skills — 79

6.1	Setting powerful heartfelt intentions	79
6.2	Writing as daily practice	85
6.3	Practising mindfulness	89
6.4	Visioning and strategy skills	91
6.5	Understanding your personality and unique gifts	93
6.6	Getting the work done (practical execution)	99
6.7	Building connection and community	105
6.8	Managing and working with opposites	110
6.9	Working with natural rhythms and cycles	112
6.10	Tuning into intuition and listening within	116
6.11	Using the power of language	123
6.12	Reading for creative influence and personal growth	125
6.13	Prioritising movement, exercise and self-care	127
6.14	Being unattached to outcomes	128
6.15	Honouring practice, ritual and experimentation	131

7. Valuing and building influences and connections — 135

7.1	Influences and creative connections: what brought you to here	135
7.2	Online creative influences and mentors	143
7.3	Finding our community	144

8. Working with the shadow side in becoming whole — 147

8.1	Exploring the shadow side	147
8.2	Wholeness, balance and shadow times in our life	150

8.3	Shadows of type: unconscious and inferior functions	152
8.4	Grief, loss and peak experiences	157
8.5	Envy and what wants to come through	159
8.6	Working with polarities	163
8.7	Choosing to shed skins	164
8.8	The cost of feeling partial and the business of the heart	165
8.9	Open-hearted change and being a work in progress	166

PART THREE — 169
BRINGING IT ALL TOGETHER

9. Guides for the wholehearted living path — 171
9.1 Synchronicity of spirit and the art of human experience — 171
9.2 Grounding in the practical and everyday — 173

10. Self-leadership and love as the heart of wholeheartedness — 175

Bibliography — 181

Quiet Writing blog posts, articles and guest posts — 185

Tarot and oracle decks and guidebooks — 187

About the Author — 189

Connecting and Sharing — 189

Endnotes — 191

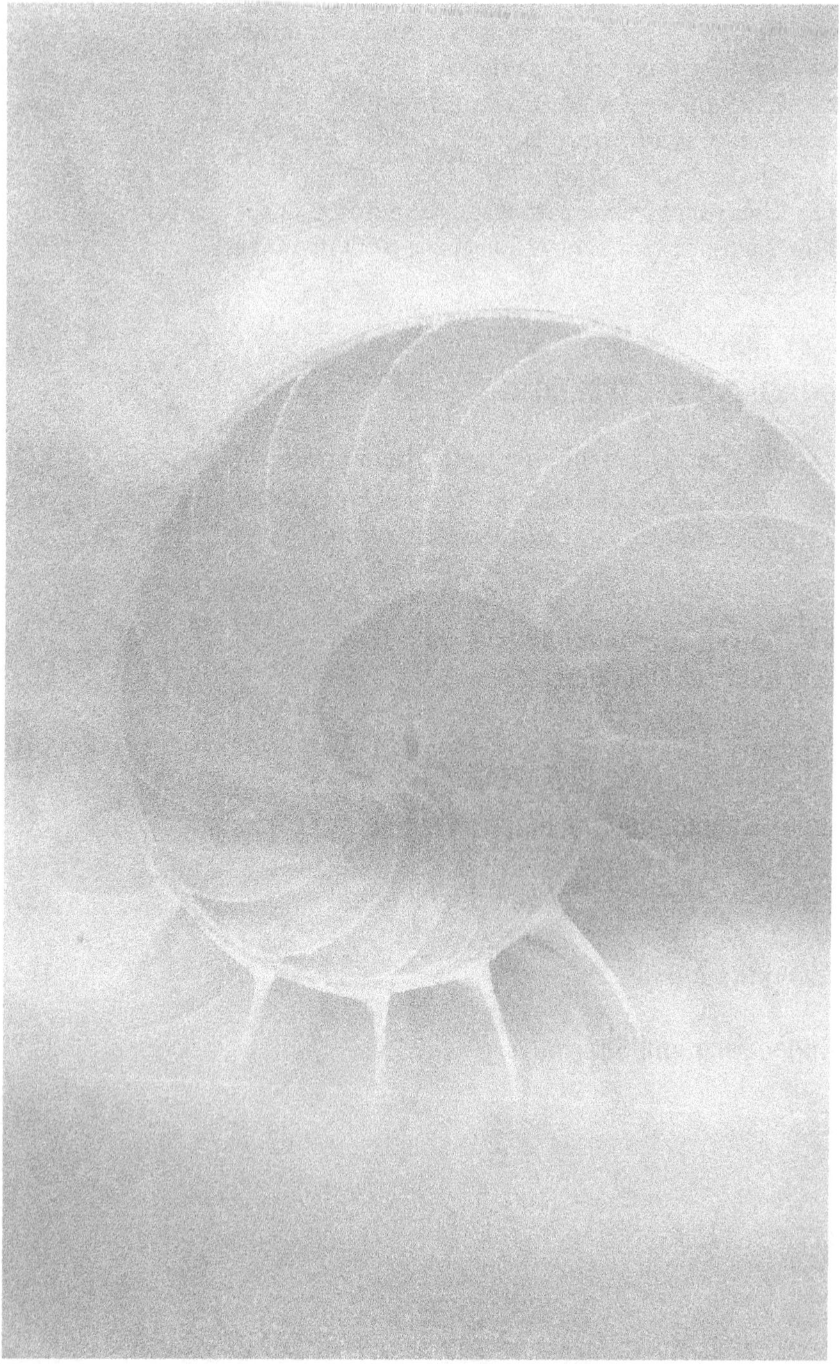

PART ONE

MY WHOLEHEARTED TRANSITION JOURNEY

1
BEGINNING THE JOURNEY

Our bodies and our personalities are vessels, and leadership, like captaincy, is full inhabitation of the vessel.

David Whyte, *Crossing the Unknown Sea*

1.1 Journey beginning

In *Wholehearted* I talk about the feelings often experienced at the beginning of a transition journey. This might involve a response to physical, emotional, mental or spiritual change or a combination of these factors. It is often a very confusing and uncertain time. Sometimes we aren't even aware we are going through a time of transition as we battle the elements of where we are and where we would like to be. The future feels like a destination that is unclear and unknown.

The imagery of transition as a journey across the water, inspired by David Whyte's book *Crossing the Unknown Sea*,[1] is a useful metaphor. Just as we can identify the language of being all at sea, being washed by waves, losing direction, to define the sensations transition creates, so we can use the metaphor of a sea journey to find solutions. We can look for anchors that can help still and ground us as we settle, find compass points and structure to give us direction, and chart the course to where we want to head day by day, dealing step by step with any challenges and obstacles that arise.

If you are beginning the journey and would like to dive deeper into Wholehearted Living Reflections to support you in this vital early stage, I invite you to reflect on Chapter 1 of *Wholehearted* through the following questions. These questions take you into a place of thinking about your experience of transition.

Space has been provided to write and record your reflections. However, you might like to start your own *Wholehearted* notebook to record your answers and write freely and fully. You might use the space below as a place to start and jot down your thoughts and then write in more detail in your own notebook. Make it a place where you can add collage, tarot cards, notes from readings, photographs, drawing and imagery and anything else that helps track and inspire your wholehearted journey of self-leadership over time.

WHOLEHEARTED LIVING REFLECTIONS

Was there a time in your life (and it might be now) when you felt like you were going on a transition journey? Write about that and describe the feelings and sensations of beginning or being in transition. Draw an image if that feels more accessible.

Think of a time when you experienced a key turning point in your transition, like the loss of a job, a change in relationship status, the death of a loved family member or friend or a move to a new home. What did it feel like in the initial stages and what transition did it foreshadow?

Did you look for footholds and places to take you forward into the future? What did these look like and how can you establish firmer footholds?

Did you need a time of withdrawal, of refuge and rescue to reorient yourself and your future? How did you carve it out then or how might you carve it out now?

1.2 In the heart of transition

I share the beginning of my transition journey in *Wholehearted*. I wonder what this aroused in you as you were reading? Jot down any thoughts or feelings here.

In times of transition, it helps to view the key journey elements and touchpoints of your life from a narrative perspective. You might ask yourself: What story is unfolding here? What stage am I at in this journey?

One of the most useful narrative structures for this exercise is the hero's journey, which has its roots in mythology and taps into universal motifs of personal transformation and adventure. Joseph Campbell explores it in detail in *The Hero with a Thousand Faces*[2] and calls it a monomyth, a story told over and over in different way with archetypal repeating elements.

There are twelve stages, clearly described in both Campbell's book and Christopher Vogler's *The Writer's Journey*. These stages and their variants inform the narrative structure of myth, life and our stories about it through creations such as novels and movies. For example, in the archetypal structure of the hero's journey, the journey often begins in the Ordinary World.

> *The Ordinary World is the context, home base, and background of the hero. The Ordinary World in one sense is the place you came from last. In life we pass through a succession of Special Worlds which slowly become ordinary as we get used to them. They evolve from strange, foreign territory to familiar bases from which to launch a drive into the next Special World.*[3]

This is where I was at in this beginning stage of my transition journey. The Ordinary World was the world of work, the daily commute, the leaving and coming home in the dark some days and the pieces of me I left behind at the door of my workplace. In my realisation that this was not where I wanted to be anymore, I began a shift to imagining Special Worlds and making them more accessible and real.

I began by imagining a future that felt so out of reach, so fantastical. In many ways it wasn't; it was about enjoying where I lived surrounded by beach and bush. It was about working from home and using my intellect in a different way. It was about getting back to where I wanted to be before making a living became the primary driving force and creativity got lost by the wayside.

Another thing that was happening in that Ordinary World was that I was becoming sick inside. All that subjugation of myself, my desires, the not stopping for lunch, the long hours, the always putting the organisation's needs first, meant that I was not looking after myself. I was not caring for myself as I should and critical things like exercise, eating well and meditative practices like yoga, swimming, walking, tarot and writing were not happening either. The weekend came and I was just too tired to do much; it was primarily devoted to resting to get up and do it all again on Monday.

Things needed to change for a whole range of reasons. Being wholehearted was not just about me, it was about others—family and friends—and about creativity and my gifts being expressed in the world. How I could share my learning, wisdom, skills in new ways to support others. I had to make changes to how I used my time and make the time for transition to a more wholehearted life.

WHOLEHEARTED LIVING REFLECTIONS

Is this how it is feeling for you also?

_____
_____
_____

Take some time to reflect on how your life is feeling now or how it felt at a time of key transition in the past. Reflecting on past transitions can also shine a light on current times. If your transition focus is the present time, use that as your framework.

_____
_____
_____
_____
_____

Where and when have you felt that life was not wholehearted for you?

What is missing? Or what was missing? Which critical parts have you left behind at the door of your life?

What passions or talents are (or were) you not deploying or living as much as you wished, trying to shoehorn them into the day or not enjoying them at all?

Do you know that feeling of knowing you were or are moving on—what are the feelings, how do they manifest?

How can you use them to imagine a different future?

_____
_____
_____
_____

What aspects reflect the Ordinary World and which aspects represent Special Worlds?

_____
_____
_____
_____
_____

1.3 Transition and Turning Points

Change is external; transition is how we respond, what happens internally. Changes can be thrust upon us or self-initiated. How we respond is within our control and where we can exert influence for more positive results and transitions.

We know from the William Bridges model that transitions often begin with endings. Something as we know it ceases to be that way and that ending becomes the source of a new beginning. There is often a turning point that characterises these transition times, a moment you can often remember very clearly that triggers or marks the turning point.

These moments are like key markers on our life journey. We know from the research work of Enz and Talarico[4] that transitions are often extended, but the turning points are more typically an event, a moment in time, often one we remember sharply. Reflecting on these turning-point moments can be instructive and powerful as turning points anchor the life story.[5]

WHOLEHEARTED LIVING REFLECTIONS

What is the transition you want to focus on for this reflection moment?

It's likely there was one turning point experience that jolted you and made you realise: this is not where I belong anymore, not the life I want to be leading. What was the turning point? Describe it factually.

Now write that experience down in as much detail as you can and feel the pain or other emotions coming through so you can move through it and on.

Taking the Bridges Transition model from 1.3 in Chapter 1 of *Wholehearted*, and particularly the idea that 'the essence of life takes place in the neutral zone phase of transition',[6] what possibilities and creative opportunities are there in the space of the neutral zone? What is beginning to surface for you from this time of transition? Or what emerged from a previous time?

_____
_____
_____
_____
_____
_____

1.4 Self-leadership: keys to wholeness and change

In 1.4, I write about how my journey as a leader also involved significant self-leadership development. I also shared about personality type and intuitive tarot practices as anchors of self-leadership in seas of change and frameworks for learning and wisdom.

Whatever path we take in life, self-leadership is emerging in different ways. We learn more about ourselves and our natural preferences. Over time, we learn to rely more on our strengths and stretch into working on our blind spots and less preferred areas. *Wholehearted* and this *Wholehearted Companion Workbook* explore this in more detail, layering as you move through it.

As a starting point in thinking about self-leadership, begin to reflect on your journey of leading yourself through what you have been through and your body of work.

WHOLEHEARTED LIVING REFLECTIONS

What have been the key learning experiences, for example work, parenting, crisis, change? What have been the major influences?

What experiences have taught you most about yourself?

What are your thoughts about self-leadership now?

What frameworks might be helpful in further developing self-knowledge and personal insights?

2

IMAGINING ANOTHER WAY

2.1 Stepping stones and lighthouses of initial inspiration and learning

Wherever you are in your transition journey, whether you feel stuck or on the way, look for your own stepping stones and lighthouses of inspiration and learning. Especially when it's hard to move immediately and you can feel frustrated, find ways to stitch practices, learning and influences into your day to keep you inspired for where you want to head.

You will possibly do this naturally, so notice what you are seeking and how. It's like following a breadcrumb trail to a vision in your heart or another version of your future, a step-by-step process you may not always recognise is happening.

Here are some reflection questions to guide your search and honouring of these stepping stones and lighthouses.

WHOLEHEARTED LIVING REFLECTIONS

What is it you want to shape for the future? Where do you want to head?

_____
_____
_____
_____

Where are you feeling stuck or frustrated, not making as much progress as you would like?

What has stayed with you? What is the enduring passion or vision or what is emerging now as a new option?

What or who might help inspire you now?

Which books are calling you and why? What podcasts might be a way to keep inspired and get new ideas? What courses might be the path?

Who are your role models for where you want to go?
What does their journey tell you for your own?

2.2 The long haul: showing up and being brave

Long-haul creativity and transition—whether that creative work is a book, a business, a new life or something else—requires us to show up and be brave over the longer term. This takes courage and it means having all kinds of practical ways to show up with courage in your toolkit.

Know too that this is not a selfish act. Self-leadership is where it starts, but each of these actions impacts and enables others. We can never know our full influence. A key part of showing up is trusting that our work makes a difference to others. Whether it's what we write, our intuitive work, social media inspiration, communicating with and caring for loved ones or holding space, it starts with each one of us but it's not all about us. It's about being of service to and inspiring others as well. We all benefit from sharing our experiences and are inspired by other's progress. It helps for us all not to hide our light in showing up or to make it appear much easier than it really is.

In *Wholehearted* I provided a list of twenty practical ways of showing up and being seen, honed from my experience and blogging[7] and shared to inspire your journey. Here they are in fuller detail for you to explore. I hope these tips inspire you to show up and be a little braver each time in all that you are doing.

As you read through, identify the ones that might apply for you by ticking the check box.

TWENTY PRACTICAL WAYS OF SHOWING UP

☐ 1 Support others who are not well or who are struggling

It might seem strange to kick off this list with a focus beyond ourselves, but supporting others and learning with them on the journey is one of the biggest and most important ways of showing up. It is easy to get caught up in our own lives, but reach out, do what you can, make time, pick up the phone, send a message or a book. Support people practically and let them know you are thinking of them.

☐ ◎ **2 Hold space for others**

Simply holding space for others—listening, witnessing, being there, asking questions—is powerful. This is something I learned through caring for my mother and my coaching practice. Having space held for me and holding it for others has been a huge support and source of growth, teaching me so much.

☐ ◎ **3 Make time for self-care**

Showing up for both yourself and others involves an investment in self-care. It might be regular practices like yoga or meditation, exercise, knowing when to rest, or making time for what lights you up. Make time for practices that energise you in line with your personality. It could be finding time to read alone if you are a more introverted person. If you are more extraverted, self-care might mean connecting with friends and going out.

A huge learning for me has been about how self-care is a critical part of caring for others. Just like the adage of putting your own oxygen mask on first, we need to feed our own wellbeing to be helpful to others. Ellen Bard's book *This Is for You: A Creative Tool-kit for Better Self-care* is a great resource with 101 creative exercises for mind, body and soul.[8]

☐ ◎ **4 Set learning goals and achieve them**

Identify learning goals that will help you reach your long-term goals and commit to them. You can set smaller goals, like spending thirty minutes each day on an online program you have invested in or working through a book to learn new skills. Choose wisely, set your learning goals and work towards them incrementally, knowing the direction.

☐ ◎ **5 Gain certification, accreditation or qualifications to strengthen your knowledge and help others**

Linked to the above, another way of showing up is to study to gain certification or qualifications. This requires commitment and working week by week over time, making sacrifices and putting in the effort, but it's so satisfying! I completed my Beautiful You Coaching Academy[9] Life Coaching program as a key part of my life transition plan and I am now a very proud Beautiful You Life Coach.

Whatever it is you need to know and develop, look at options to gain the skills you need. They can be in formal or less formal ways; both are important options to consider. Don't be afraid of the more formal path and what it offers.

☐ ◉ 6 Honour your personality and deepen your gifts

Honour your special natural attributes and skills, by recognising them, paying attention to them and investing in them. Find out more about your personality and how to work your strengths.[10] Personality-wise, it could be introversion or extraversion, sensing or intuition, thinking or feeling. Talent-wise, it might be writing, photography, knitting or art. For example, I learned more about tarot as a way of honouring my personality and deepening my gift of Introverted Intuiting.[11] Susannah Conway's *78 Mirrors* course and my own ongoing practice helped me deepen my knowledge of tarot as an intuitive tool.

☐ ◉ 7 Develop your gifts and talents by practising them consistently

Once you've identified your strengths and talents, one of the best ways to show up is to practise them. Tarot and oracle have become deep personal practices that I work with regularly, flexing my intuition. I share my *Tarot Narratives* regularly on Instagram as a way of practising and showing up for myself and others. If you are working on writing, show up by writing each day. It might be Morning Pages, a set number of words, an amount of time or a unit that makes sense to you. But whatever it is, put it into practice. As Stephen King reminds us:

> *Talent is a dreadfully cheap commodity, cheaper than table salt. What separates the talented individual from the successful one is a lot of hard work and study; a constant process of honing.*[12]

☐ 8 Connect on social media as a way of showing up and practice

Social media gets a bad rap as a time waster. It's true, you can waste a lot of time there if you are unfocused. But connecting on social media can be a beautiful way to show up for yourself and your creativity. It can also be powerful in supporting and helping others. I've shown up on social media over time because I value it immensely as a way of connecting with kindred creatives, growing the Quiet Writing community and learning from my connections. Whether it's sharing creative practices, books, tarot readings, the detail around you or the landscapes or streetscapes of your environment—it's all a way of expressing you.

☐ 9 Commit to blogging, reading or other accountability practices regularly

As a creative, you can show up via commitment to a pattern of accountable, regular practice. Showing up has an aspect of accountability. It might be books read on Goodreads, blog posts on your blog, social media over time or working quietly with an accountability group behind the scenes.

I have blogged for over ten years now but at times have struggled with consistency. In my pivotal transition year, I posted once or twice each week. It was a challenge but I committed to it and that helped me find my voice. Reading can also be an exercise in accountability and productivity practice.[13] Try to find a practice and metric that works for you and be accountable.

☐ 10 Write about your story

Be authentic and write your story. This helps others feel less alone and encourages them to do the same. I have written about my journey of becoming more wholehearted on Quiet Writing, encouraging others to do so too. From that, I've encouraged other women to share their *Wholehearted Stories*[14] with more than twenty women coming forward to guest post on Quiet Writing since 2017. Each story opens the door for others and helps them to discover and share their own story. It might be a blog post, a novel, a poem or a memoir. Telling your story will help you work out so much— just as it will help others to read your experiences.

☐ 🐚 11 Write for others, guest post and stretch your voice and audiences

Embrace your ability to draw on your experiences and knowledge to write for others such as via guest posting or being interviewed on podcasts. It's a way of showing up because you have to ask yourself: What do I know? What have I experienced? What can I share? How can I help others?

It pushes your boundaries, stretches you and helps make connections across areas of your knowledge, skills and experience. Powerful stuff, it makes you more visible and builds your audience as well. As an example, here's a post I originally wrote as a guest post on a subject dear to my heart: leadership, self-leadership and solitude.[15]

☐ 🐚 12 Write and publish or self-publish

Write with a view to publishing, whether it be on your blog, for a publisher or self-publishing. It's all valid and more than that, is a path to ways of earning income, developing your voice and getting your work out there. Independent publishing is not vanity publishing anymore; it is a very real way to be read and to reach people and to build business, skill and revenue. As Joanna Penn says on publishing options:

> *The publishing world is exploding with opportunity ... and many authors are finding new ways to build a career with self-publishing, traditional publishing or a hybrid combination of the two.*[16]

☐ 🐚 13 Communicate and connect with others, especially kindred creatives

Connect with special kindred souls whether it be via your newsletter, in social media exchanges or through sharing posts and books. Create ways people can communicate with you and be accessible if your aim is visibility. People want to connect with you as a creative human being in whatever way you can make that work for you and others.

If you do find someone who you connect with as a kindred creative, reach out to them in some way. You may feel vulnerable, but it's worth the risk. You never know what might evolve from showing up in this way. Some of my best collaborations and connections have developed from one of us doing exactly that!

☐ ◐ 14 Commit to working on energy healing and spiritual areas

Working on energy healing and spiritual development is integral to personal growth and self-care. I've committed to working on my intuitive skills as well as healing and working with guides to support my growth and creativity including working with the magical energetic healer Amber Adrian.[17]

Find what works for you in energy and spiritual realms. Whether it's prayer, angels, crystals, tarot, oracle, channelling, astrology or the cycles of the moon, working with these connections is supportive in managing our energy, healing, breaking through barriers and being authentic. And work on shedding any concerns about what people think about this. It's time for us all to come out of the spiritual closet.

☐ ◐ 15 Work with a coach

Working with a coach is a fabulous way to show up for yourself and others. Coaching is goal-driven and action-oriented. You are in the driver's seat and are responsible for showing up and doing the actions. You can have an excellent coach, but unless you do the work, there won't be much personal progress. But showing up for your coaching work, whether it's one on one or in a group context where you are also showing up for others, is powerful and deep work. It often helps to have a guide for those areas that feel challenging or where you need accountability.

☐ 🐚 **16 Connect with family members including through family history research**

Making time for family and ancestry is a way of showing up for yourself and others you are connected with over time. Spend time hearing or learning about the stories. My family and family history are important. I'm committed to understanding the stories of my family including the people who came before me. This helps to keep family, family history research and ancestral connections alive and can teach you so much about yourself and your heritage.

☐ 🐚 **17 Work with or for other people in line with your values**

Whether it's paid, pro bono, volunteer, in the home or outside, how are you working with or for other people? How do the experiences and outcomes validate you and show that you are on the right path and have much to give? If it's not feeling right, how else could you work with and for other people to grow in a different direction? Think about how you are aligned or how you can be better aligned so you can show up for what is of value to you.

☐ 🐚 **18 Work through the practicalities of health and wellbeing issues**

Our health is an evolving and changing issue and one we need to honour and show up around, whether in public or private ways. There's no point putting your head in the sand about your health—physical, emotional and mental health. You don't have to share what's not comfortable but on the flip side, if we all stay quiet, what is the impact of this?

Consider: How are you showing up on the health issues in your life and how are you addressing them? How are you taking responsibility for any changes and understanding them? What actions are you taking? What support is there? How can you connect with others and with information on health issues? Are you reaching out for help if you need it? How are you showing up for others?

As well as caring for my mother in my transition time, I was diagnosed with the autoimmune disease Hashimoto's thyroiditis as well as osteoarthritis. I'm also asthmatic and suffered severe attacks for a time. Working through the practicalities of all this with medical and health practitioners, I've made dietary and exercise changes that have made a world of difference.

☐ 🐚 **19 Identify your body of work in the world**

Whether it's the job you are in now or the job you are heading to or if you are self-employed or working for others, identify your skills and body of work in the world. Consider: How have you shown up over time in roles and with skills that matter? How have you made a difference? What are the special skills you bring to the world? Think about how you can develop and take this body of work forward to help others.

☐ 🐚 **20 Identify the core themes in your business or life's work**

I've worked on my Quiet Writing business and its core concepts—its focus, key tenets, proposed offerings, how I can serve people. I know its focus is 'wholehearted self-leadership' based on my own experiences. Being connected, creative, flowing, intuitive and poetic are core values of my brand.

Consider: What are the core themes in your business or life's work? What are the threads that tie this story together? How can you serve others from all that you have learned? Think about how you can show up in your business or creativity to help others.

WHOLEHEARTED LIVING REFLECTIONS

Now look at what you have ticked above and identify your top three ways of showing up to work on:

1. _____

2. _____

3. _____

Now identify an action plan to put this into place.
What will you start doing?

_____
_____

What will you stop doing?

_____
_____

How are you showing up in the world?

_____
_____

Where have you stretched a little this past year to show up, hold space, reach out, learn, put your creative work into the world?

_____
_____

When you have showed up and been vulnerable, how did it help others?

_____
_____

How could you be a little braver?

_____
_____

Where would it be of benefit to show up more?

_____
_____

How could you showing up more be helpful to others?

2.3 Hard inner work, not luck

In 2.3 I share insights from my friend, writer and teacher Kerstin Pilz,[18] and my own experiences about the role of luck versus hard inner work in our personal development. Our own privilege and the situations we find ourself in play a role in our circumstances and this is valuable to consider, work through and understand. But often way too much emphasis is placed on luck as if it is the only determinant. Working on ourselves, skilling up, making wise choices, showing up and dealing with all the kinds of resistance that arise are all critical parts of self-leadership and hard inner work.

WHOLEHEARTED LIVING REFLECTIONS

Did you relate to Kerstin Pilz's story in 2.3 of *Wholehearted*?

What are your thoughts about the role of luck versus hard work?

Look at issues of privilege in your life through connecting with the work of leadership and inclusion coach Sharyn Holmes.[19]

SELF-LEARNING GOALS

I also share the self-learning goals that were the pillars for my transition path. They emerged fairly intuitively and were beacons for the next phase of my life, for the transition and transformation. Learning goals can be very powerful anchors and ways of focusing hard inner work as part of making a significant life change.

WHOLEHEARTED LIVING REFLECTIONS

What are your self-learning goals to guide your inner work path?

_____
_____
_____

How do they connect with each other and what might they bring forth?

_____
_____
_____

2.4 How our self-talk guides and shapes us as we imagine a new way

In this section of *Wholehearted*, I shared some very personal and painful insights about when I first learnt about how self-talk can create or keep us in situations and how we can work consciously with self-talk and the language we choose to find a way out and shape a new path.

I hope it wasn't too painful for you if you have been or are going through anything like this. But I think situations like this—domestic violence, power over others, the gender and racial reasons behind such behaviour, what it manifests in victims—need to be talked about where we can. So much continues because of silence and I know personally how easy it is to stay silent because of shame.

WHOLEHEARTED LIVING REFLECTIONS

What came up for you as you read through this?

Was there any particular situation you have been through where you have learnt the power of self-talk and the language we use internally? What were the learnings? Where did you shift?

LIMITING SELF-BELIEFS

Negative self-talk also is an indicator of limiting self-beliefs—what we feel we are worth, what stories we may have picked up and perpetuate via our family or socially about our perceived value, what upper limits we might be placing on ourselves as Gay Hendricks describes it in *The Big Leap*.[20]

WHOLEHEARTED LIVING REFLECTIONS

What words or phrases might be indicators of any limiting self-beliefs in the language that you use?

_____
_____
_____
_____
_____

How might you choose different words or take action to remind yourself of the power of the words that you use in everyday life?

_____
_____
_____
_____
_____

There are many ways we can consciously use language positively to guide our personal self-leadership journey and we explore this more in 6.11. Think affirmations, intentions and setting a word of the year as examples.

What comes to mind now as ways you can use language and self-talk particularly to step into a new version and vision of you?

_____
_____
_____
_____
_____

3

IDENTIFYING YOUR PASSIONS AND WHAT YOU LOVE

3.1 Why identify your passions?

In Chapter 3, I share why I think identifying your passions is key to self-leadership. We often take for granted the things and people we love and are drawn to and don't take the time to reflect on why. Therein lie powerful insights into our uniqueness and how we can use that information as insights for positive transition.

WHOLEHEARTED LIVING REFLECTIONS

What are your thoughts on why it's important to identify our passions?

_____
_____

What might they tell us?

_____
_____

3.2 Qualities of passions

In *Wholehearted*, we identified three qualities and dimensions as clues to identifying the passions and loves that define us. Here is a deeper dive into these three areas. I take you through examples of my passions in each area and how I noticed, discovered and connected them more deeply. I invite you to explore and document your passions as a foundation for transition. This will help you feel more strongly rooted in what you love as you grow and change.

1. The superpower or authentic centrepieces

We are often aware of these central passions but can work more consciously with them as an anchor of familiarity and source of growth, especially in times of transition. These ones are fairly easy to spot. They are what you say when someone asks you about your superpower or strength. They are the enduring passions and loves you go back to again and again as a touchstone, especially at tough times. They are the stuff of dreams and plans: writing a book, travelling to a place, being with that special someone, being a poet/chef/designer/author—you insert your special one.

If anyone asks me what my superpower is, it is writing. I'm a word wrangler from way back and I have written diaries, poetry, journal articles, ministerial speeches, reports, media releases, blog posts, strategic documents. And the special thing I aspire to be in my life? A writer, an author, a poet, a published author, an indie author. All of these please.

The other passion that backs up my writing superpowers is reading. I love books, reading and creative influence, and I've been a teacher of literacy, such is my passion for imparting the skill and love of reading and writing to others.

Another huge passion is time alone, solitude, space to think and create, walking on the beach, in the bush, swimming. As you can see it is no surprise my website and business is called *Quiet Writing*. This coalesces my key passions in a real way.

WHOLEHEARTED LIVING REFLECTIONS

So think, what are your key passions, your top three?

1. _____

2. _____

3. _____

How do they coalesce into the brand or essence of you?

_____
_____
_____
_____
_____
_____
_____

2. **The things we love we might not immediately think of as passions— the people, the books, the types of narratives, what we love to do.**

Another key way to get insights into your passions is to look at what you love—the people, the books, the animals, the experiences—and see the consistent themes running through.

The people you connect with and who light you up can provide an insight into your passions. Ask yourself: What qualities are you drawn to? What are you seeking in being drawn to them? Are they well-read? Are they practical? Are they things you seek for yourself or are you trying to balance your own personality? These in themselves can be clues to what you are seeking in life focused on what you love.

WHOLEHEARTED LIVING REFLECTIONS

What clues arrive for you now?

_____
_____
_____

What do the grand passions of your life tell you? Who did you fall head over heels for, even if your love was not reciprocated or requited? Why was that? What part of the passionate inner self did this bring to life? Or were you looking to solve a problem or complement a side of yourself?

_____
_____
_____
_____

Another clue to these more hidden and second-order passions is our hobbies and bookshelves. My exploration in my book *Reading as Creative Influence*[21] was a journey through the books that have been the biggest creative influences in my life. It was like a trail of crumbs I followed that told me so much about what I love, including what I hadn't properly realised or given a rightful place. (More on this in 6.12.)

What is it that you love to do when times get tough?

_____
_____
_____

What have been enduring values and loves over time?

_____
_____

What books on your bookshelves are evidence of what you love?

---

3. **The forgotten passions, the secret passions—those that we love and may not have acknowledged, or that we have buried or forgotten.**

Sometimes our passions and loves become forgotten or buried for some reason, and it may take time and work to uncover them. We might have left them behind because of perceived social acceptability or someone else's preferences. Or perhaps our secret passions are an unlived part of us wanting to break through.

I had a fascinating experience listening to Joanna Penn and AK Benedict in a podcast on *Writing the Darkness*[22] where they shared their love of dark things and writing about them. Cemeteries, gravestones, spooky places, murders, dark arts and practices. They talked about how their families wondered where they had gone wrong and how it is something they have come to accept in themselves despite the perception of others. It made me think about parts of my life that I had left behind or passions I had not talked about or indulged in because they felt wrong somehow.

As a child, I loved ghost stories and classic horror movies— *Frankenstein*, *Dracula*, *The Time Machine* with Rod Taylor and the Morlocks, *The Birds* with Tippi Hedren. My favourite author is Daphne du Maurier. I love her dark psychological thrillers, *Rebecca* being my favourite book. Reading Sydney author Karina Machado's book *Spirit Sisters* about Australian women's experience with the paranormal fascinated and enthralled me.

So these threads suggest a passion for what exactly? Darker sides of life, human experience, the psychology of this, the unusual, the paranormal, the mysterious. It took some realising and probably because I'd shut it off, perhaps in fear. But it is okay to have passions that are a little dark, interests that are a touch macabre, you never know where they might lead or how the connections may come together. You never know the true story of this passion and love until you dive into it.

Leaving it to gather dust is not going to help. As I've come to terms with and revisited my love of ghost stories, I'm discovering that this passion is teaching me more about what I'd like to write.

A love of spiritual and intuitive areas might indicate what you are drawn to that you can be dismissive of or guarded about. My love of tarot has been a journey through this terrain. Many people with a mystical or psychic bent can feel it is something that needs to be hidden, at least till they begin to come to terms with it, often for social reasons, wondering what others will think. So seek deep into your more hidden and secret passions and see what light they might shed on what you love or find intriguing. You never know what you might find.

WHOLEHEARTED LIVING REFLECTIONS

What comes to mind for you as secret or hidden passions?

What did you love as a child that perhaps got left behind?

Are there any emerging or re-emerging passions that you are feeling more private? What do they tell you about yourself?

3.3 Finding your authentic heart

In *Wholehearted* I share about the value of finding, knowing and being clear on your authentic heart, what matters the most to you. Here are a few more clues and tips for discovering and exploring your most genuine centrepiece based on my experience. I encourage you to explore and get clear on yours.

CLUES FOR DISCOVERING AND EXPLORING YOUR PASSIONS

So what were the key themes and passions in my life, my shortlist for the authentic heart of me?

- **A love of reading and the language arts** which I pursued to masters degree level. From this I learnt how to read classic and modern texts in depth and analytically, and how to write about them with research, structure and argument to match.
- **A love of writing** which I wove through everything I did from teaching and communicating it to learning how to wield the sword of its mighty power. I sharpened my skills every day in all the different writing I did from essays to poetry to blogs, to political papers to policy statements to briefings for government ministers to strategic vision documents. I honoured the spirit of writing in my life as my authentic heart each day and kept its spirit alive.
- **A love of personal narrative and personality** through leadership, self-leadership, leading others, leading teams, reading novels, reading self-help books, going to university and gaining degrees, reading about Jung, learning about my personality and that of the people I led so we could work together well as a team and make a difference. I learnt to exercise self-leadership in senior leadership roles and in the pressure of the political arena where everything you do has higher stakes and visibility.

Over time too I did the hard inner work in a parallel journey to the workplace one. It all came together in the universe of me and it all made a difference to my body of work. But it was quieter, inner work of blogging, building a website, working out what I stood for, and what my brand was, realising what I loved and valued and knowing what I wanted to learn.

I connected with people who were also blazing trails like this. Susannah Conway, who wrote a book and built a blog and creative business out of the broken-hearted grief of suddenly losing the love of her life. Joanna Penn, who knew that she wanted to write books and see them out in the world and carved a new entrepreneurial life for herself, and who bravely started a podcast on creativity, writing and self-publishing when hardly anybody knew what a podcast was, and who has spearheaded an independent publishing path to self-employment.[23]

And friends like my creative friend, Victoria Smith, who I met through *Blogging from the Heart,* who was on a similar journey though a few steps ahead, leaving her day job by degrees after not feeling wholehearted from working so hard in ways that did not align with her authentic heart.

Those people one or a few steps ahead of us in wholehearted self-leadership and creativity are such golden role models we can learn from. When the day came for my moment of crisis when it all came to a head and I had to regroup and plan another way, it was Victoria I reached out to for help. I knew her journey through wholehearted self-leadership could help me on my own journey.

WHOLEHEARTED LIVING REFLECTIONS

What key themes emerge for you as the central ones in your life?

What clues are there in the lives of others you follow and learn from?

PRACTICAL STRATEGIES FOR DISCOVERING YOUR AUTHENTIC HEART

Here are some practical strategies for discovering your authentic heart. Identify the ones that will be the most helpful for you now.

☐ 🐚 **1. Journalling, Morning Pages, dialoguing with the self**

Make time for journalling, Morning Pages or any other form of writing to tap into your inner voice. That ability to hear your voice on the page and settle yourself is the source of so much wisdom. The solitude afforded is in itself is a valuable teacher.

☐ 🐚 **2. Working with a coach**

Working with a coach is a valuable way to be supported in hearing your inner voice. A coach holds space for you, asks questions to enable reflection, and suggests resources and options to help make change. This gift of personal investment enables powerful discovery and behaviour change in line with your goals. Coaching can be one-to-one or in a group context such as the Sacred Creative Collective Group Coaching that I offer.[24] Both have advantages: one-to-one coaching is intensive and customised solely to you; group coaching has the benefit of community and learning from and connecting with others as you create the work of your heart or commence or negotiate a transition.

☐ 🌀 **3. Reflecting on the threads that recur in your body of work**

Identifying the threads that reappear in your life's work across its manifestations is a valuable way to reflect on your journey and story. As Pamela Slim defines in her book *Body of Work*, your body of work is all that you create over time and your legacy. Taking this broader view of all your contributions and creations enables you to step back and see the passions that drive you. You can identify the common connections and from this, achieve a new perspective on life, career and creativity options. You can reflect more on your body of work in section 5 of this workbook.

☐ 🌀 **4. Thinking about your shadow career**

As Steven Pressfield explains in *Turning Pro*, sometimes when we are afraid of our real calling we will follow a shadow career instead. Explore this concept to find out what this might tell you about what you value and desire. This might mean living the writer's lifestyle without actually writing or writing in a corporate context when you really want to be writing a novel.

As Pressfield says:

> *If you're dissatisfied with your current life, ask yourself what your current life is a metaphor for. That metaphor will point you to your true calling.*[25]

☐ 🌀 **5. Thinking about the books you love as clues and evidence**

Think about the books you love as a form of evidence. Look at your bookshelves. What's the predominant story and style? What's the genre? Has it been lost along the way? What ignites your heart? See my book, *Reading as Creative Influence*,[26] for inspiration about how the books we love can be a trail to wisdom and insight. Explore your own creative influence trail from the ideas therein. Journal about what comes up for you.

☐ 6. Brainstorming, lists and visual maps to find the common threads

Mind-mapping, journalling, vision boards, Pinterest, brainstorming and writing lists are all valuable tools to get to the common threads of your work. Work with various options for diverse perspectives. Different options rely on and activate different parts of the brain and personality preferences. Mix it up so you can access alternative angles.

If you are a visually oriented person, for example, work with what comes naturally for you, like Pinterest or mind-mapping to bring up new and fresh ways of seeing and tapping into the unconscious. Then shift into your less preferred area to write a more logical and objective list. And vice versa, if you are more rational and list-oriented, try working with collage. See your work from a number of views to uncover the golden threads that connect in new ways.

☐ 7. Intuitive writing and work such as tarot or oracle to tap into your inner voice

Activate and tap into your inner wisdom via working with tarot and oracle cards. Intuitive writing, journal writing, free writing or any other stream-of-consciousness approach is another way to access your intuition. Regularly making time for the practice of intuition in whatever works for you helps you tune into your creative energies. Tristine Rainer's *The New Diary*[27] has some powerful intuitive journal writing strategies.

☐ 8. Writing down what your ideal day looks and feels like

Writing what your ideal day looks like is an excellent activity for insight into what you really want. Often we find as we do this over time, the core threads are surprisingly consistent. Find out how you truly want to spend your time. This helps you recognise when you start to get glimpses of it or finally achieve a measure of success. You might have already achieved your ideal day in some respects and be ready to set some new visions of what an ideal day in a few years' time looks like.

☐ 🐚 **9. Tuning into what others are saying about you and your gifts**

Tune into the many clues from what people say about us, so you can fully listen and take their insights on board. What are others saying they appreciate about you: your calmness, your ability to listen, your creativity, how they relate to your writing, how organised you are, your use of colour? Pay attention to feedback, keep a record and notice what is being reflected to you as insight into your gifts and purpose.

WHOLEHEARTED LIVING REFLECTIONS

Finding your authentic heart is about naming the passion that kindles your fire and opening to it. So what is your authentic heart? What is the practice, the creative work, the combining principle, the thread that ties it all together?

_____
_____
_____
_____
_____

3.4 The unique voice of what you love: your onlyness

Round off thinking about your authentic heart and your onlyness from the ideas in Chapter 3 further here.

WHOLEHEARTED LIVING REFLECTIONS

Where are you keeping a light in your heart?

What are the beacons in your day showing the way back to?

What shadows are showing up? What are they highlighting?

What is the authentic centrepiece for you?

Why is it the centrepiece—how does it connect other passions and loves?

What key aspects combine to make up your onlyness?

What makes your special blend unique? Where are the unusual combining elements that make up you?

_____
_____
_____

Formulate a powerful question about your onlyness. Write it here.

_____
_____
_____

Seek insights on this question by choosing a tarot or oracle reading for insights into your onlyness and uniqueness. Journal about what comes up.

_____
_____
_____
_____

4

IDENTIFYING YOUR NATURAL GIFTS, STYLE AND DESIRES

Create your own style ... let it be unique for yourself and yet identifiable for others.

Anna Wintour

4.1 The examined life

In *Wholehearted* I talk about the difference between living on the surface of your life and living a more examined life where you are more aware of personal drivers, how you are wired, what makes you 'you' and how you might express that in language to describe yourself including to others. There is nature and nurture at play as always but what we naturally prefer, how our brain is configured, is a huge factor and one we can work more actively to understand in a self-compassionate way.

We can get into the unconscious habit of beating ourselves up just because we are different. We might be a more unusual personality type such as being a woman with Thinking preferences when women are stereotypically and numerically more likely to have a preference for Feeling. You might feel like the odd one out in your own home or family—an introvert in a family of extraverts, for example.

Enough beating ourselves up because we are different. Let us find out more about the beautiful person we are and how we tick and work with ourselves rather than against our natural grain. Polishing our own strengths and learning to value them and work with them can be one of the most valuable things we can do.

Before we dive in more fully, take a moment to reflect on your self-knowledge now.

WHOLEHEARTED LIVING REFLECTIONS

How would you describe how well you know yourself right now?

Do you have a sense of how you are wired?

Do you know what drives you and leads you, what defines you and why?

4.2 Personality type and preferences

In *Wholehearted*, I share how knowing about my psychological type preferences has made all the difference in my life in understanding myself and accepting myself as I am. It is also a powerful foundation on which to build personal development and a framework for knowing and valuing our strengths as well as our less preferred areas.

Carl Jung first published his work on psychological types in 1921. On the basis of his work with patients, Jung describes two attitudes - Extraversion and Introversion - and the four functions of Intuiting, Sensing, Thinking and Feeling that make up the heart of psychological type:

> *In this way, we can orientate ourselves with respect to the immediate world as completely as when we locate a place geographically by latitude and longitude. The four functions are somewhat like the four points of the compass; they are just as arbitrary and just as indispensable ...*
> *But one thing I must confess: I would not for anything dispense with this compass on my psychological journeys of discovery.*[28]

This is the value of psychological type—as a compass to help us orientate ourselves, get our bearings, describe how we are operating, what feels natural and what feels less natural for us and realising where we may be operating more unconsciously and less skilfully.

We all have our own personal cognitive framework or compass. Katharine Briggs and Isabel Myers described a system of sixteen types, developed on the basis of Jung's work. You may know your type or have heard of them; examples include INFJ and ESTP. And many others have contributed to this rich field of insight over time.

The letters refer to your preference from a pair of preferences, such as E or I Extraversion or Introversion, S or N Sensing or Intuition (with an N used for Intuition). The preferences combine to make up a dynamic personality type. Here's a primer of the pairs of preferences and what they mean from Mary McGuiness's fabulous book on psychological type, *You've Got Personality*.[29]

The four pairs of preferences

What is the direction and focus of your personal energy?	**E Extraversion** A preference for the outer world of people, events, activity and things.	**I Introversion** A preference for the inner world of ideas, thoughts, feelings and impressions.
How do you prefer to gather information?	**S Sensing** Focus on past or present experience, what is experienced through the senses.	**N iNtuition** Focus on patterns, future possibilities and the meaning behind ideas.
How do you prefer to make decisions?	**T Thinking** Use logic to make decisions. Base decisions on laws and principles or logical analysis.	**F Feeling** Weigh values to make decisions. Decide what is most important for people.
How do you deal with the outer world?	**J Judging** Prefer to be planned and organised in the outer world, seeking closure.	**P Perceiving** Prefer to be spontaneous and flexible in the outer world, ready to explore new options.

Table reproduced from *You've Got Personality* by Mary McGuiness with the permission of the author.

You can see how working from our preferences is a lens on how we see, experience and process the world and how working from one frame of preferences might put you at odds with others too!

WHOLEHEARTED LIVING REFLECTIONS

Do you know your psychological type? (For example ISTP or ENFJ.)

If so, what does that mean for you? In what context did you learn this? How confident do you feel about that and how well do you understand yourself using this framework?

If not, have a look at the preference pairs and get a beginning sense of where your preferences might lie.

4.3 Understanding our preferences and gifts

In *Wholehearted* I share my experience of getting clearer on my psychological type and preferences. There are many psychological type lenses and frameworks that can help with understanding your preferences and specific gifts.

Building on the ideas in the previous section, a key aspect of looking at your psychological type preferences is based on Jung's original 1921 work.[30] It is about gaining insight into the cognitive processes that you naturally prefer. There are four functions: Sensing, Intuition, Thinking and Feeling, and each of the four functions can be used in the internal or external world, that is, in an extraverted or introverted way. So we end up with eight Jungian functions as follows and described by Mary McGuiness in *You've Got Personality*.[31]

There are **four perceiving functions** about how we gather information, described as follows with the frequently used abbreviations.

- Extraverted Sensing—Sensory experience (Se)
- Extraverted Intuition—Exploring possibilities (Ne)
- Introverted Sensing—Sensory memory (Si)
- Introverted Intuition—Visionary insight (Ni)

There are **four judging functions** about how we process information or make decisions:

- Extraverted Thinking—Logical outcomes (Te)
- Extraverted Feeling—Harmonizing people (Fe)
- Introverted Thinking—Internal analysis (Ti)
- Introverted Feeling—Universal values (Fi)

We each have a dominant, preferred function from these eight functions that gives us insight into the leadership of our personality.

Neuroscience research by Dario Nardi[32] has helped to see exactly what the brain is doing when it carries out certain types of tasks and how this relates to psychological type. As a person with INTJ preferences, my dominant, preferred function is Introverted Intuiting or Visionary insight, and tarot especially helps me hone and trust this gift.

Dario Nardi's book *8 Keys to Self-leadership*[33] takes you through a detailed journey of each of the eight functions as a set of cognitive tools you can use. The framework of functions helps you see where you are strongest and where you might have weaknesses or blind spots. This also helps see where you might naturally align or clash with others and can build skill and awareness including positively addressing potential conflict points with others.

Other type lenses include the Temperament framework presented in David Keirsey's book *Please Understand Me II*[34] and Interaction Styles constructs that help explain our natural interacting preferences and how and why we might encounter challenges with others. Excellent resources for further exploring this area are: *How to Get on with Anyone* by Catherine Stothart[35] and *Understanding Yourself and Others* by Linda V Berens.[36]

WHOLEHEARTED LIVING REFLECTIONS

Make some notes here about what you know and what to learn about your personality and psychological type.
What do you know or believe about your personality and psychological type now from previous experience or from reading the above?

_____
_____

What would you like to explore further?

_____
_____

What is the action plan for making this happen?

_____
_____

Note that this is just a preliminary check-in. Working on understanding your type is important work requiring background learning and is best done with the support of a skilled, accredited coach. It's a very deep well of knowledge, learning and insight and a valuable guide for self-leadership and much more than just the eight Jungian functions, though they are a valuable start. We work on it a little more in the next section too.

I offer programs that include self-paced ecourses and coaching so that you can know your psychological type and work with it in a deep way.[37] And I weave this knowledge into everything I do!

4.4 Quiet, quiet leadership and our personal brand of strength

I share in *Wholehearted* about truly discovering how to tap into the power of my quieter side as a source of strength rather than as a weakness. It's amazing how our very strengths can feel like weaknesses, especially the quieter ones that are not as valued in a more extraverted world.

Explore some of these strengths and how they might feel like weaknesses. There are also some tips on how to honour them and not overuse them.

Strengths	How it might feel like or be seen as a weakness	How to honour and value and not overuse
Introversion and quietness	Not speaking up, being slow to respond, being aloof or disconnected	Learn to value quieter ways of working and influencing. Understand what you need to do to recharge and prepare and honour that. Identify ways you can provide responses and connect in your own way, e.g. via writing or one on one.
Listening	Being seen as passive rather than active, not being seen as a contributor	Value the much-underrated art of listening as much as the skill of speaking. Notice where your listening skills hold space for others and help them to reflect and listen within. Seek out opportunities to develop and apply your listening skills, e.g. coaching, one-on-one conversation.

Gaining energy via respite and retreat	Seen as not being a team player, antisocial or unavailable	Acknowledge and value your need for respite and retreat as a source of strength and insight. Read case studies on how this can be powerfully enacted and why it is important for all—introverts and extraverts.[38] Realise that leading yourself first is a prerequisite to leading others and this might mean taking time out for clarity and reflection Focus on how you might communicate this need to others so they understand it.

These are just a few ideas to get you thinking about quieter strengths and how they can be valued and recast.

WHOLEHEARTED LIVING REFLECTIONS

Do any of these quieter strengths resonate with you? Or do you have your own examples?

_____
_____

What experiences have you had of these quieter strengths being seen as negative, or feeling them to be so?

_____
_____

What other strengths might be underrated, including more extraverted strengths?

_____
_____

How can you honour them positively in your life?
What's your personal action plan?

_____

_____

_____

_____

4.5 Your unique style, Style Statement and Style Type

In *Wholehearted* I share how working on a *Style Statement* can be a valuable way of understanding the key drivers of your style and creativity in the world. It is a fundamental perspective that continues to guide me and my work in the world.

I have created a Pinterest Board of my *Sacred Creative* Style Statement[39] and I've kept adding to it over the years. The images there are like windows into my soul. Sometimes I still struggle to understand the full meaning of *Sacred Creative*; it is a transformative phrase, one I can continue to grow into and aspire to especially as I move between worlds in a state of becoming.

Possible Style Statements are myriad and examples include: Current Sensual, Innovative Feminine, Enduring Bold, Designed Ease, Genuine Legacy. Each one evokes such imagery. You can create one that you connect with deeply as a guiding force for transition and as an anchor for your heart. We also looked at how style can relate to type through the 16 Style Types[40] work of Jill Chivers, Jane Kise and Imogen Lamport as another valuable perspective on our unique style.

WHOLEHEARTED LIVING REFLECTIONS

What steps will you take next in exploring the resources mentioned in this chapter?

Which areas call to you from these resources to explore first?

What would you define as your natural gifts?

What two-word statement comes to mind when you think of your style? Record it here or play around with ideas and words that come to you now to describe the essence of you, your style and how you would like to design your life.

Work through the *Style Statement* book[41] and come up with your unique Style Statement. I assure you it is worth the time and is a beautiful experience of discovery and clarification.

Create a Pinterest board focused on your Style Statement to explore it in deeper ways and for visual and creative inspiration.

Explore the 16 Style Types resources. How do you think your style links to your personality type?

4.6 Your Core Desired Feelings

The Core Desired Feelings identified via Danielle LaPorte's *The Desire Map*[42] process have been another anchor and framework for how I want to feel in the work that I do in the world. These feelings once clarified can be a wonderful touchstone for what is right for you and what is not right for you. They can also help you convey how you desire others to feel in their interactions with you and what you invite in their lives. And you can keep revisiting to revise them as you grow and change.

As I developed *Quiet Writing* as a business and brand, my core desired feelings were the keywords I chose to introduce Quiet Writing concepts on the Welcome page in September 2016.[43] They defined how I wanted to feel and also what I invited my readers and coaching and personality clients to feel, while negotiating major life transitions.

Here's a summary of my core desired feelings and what they mean to me:

Creative—open, exploring, expressing creativity, living creatively
Connected—with self, with others, grounded, networked, connecting ideas and people together to innovate and create opportunities
Flowing—at peace, writing to discover, moving with ease through transition
Intuitive—working with intuition as a guide, learning intuitive practices and tools such as tarot, oracle, writing, to support transition and creativity
Poetic—inspired by language, possibility, words, lyricism, beauty

WHOLEHEARTED LIVING REFLECTIONS

How could you use how you want to feel as a guide to the vision for your life?

Work through *The Desire Map* book and identify your Core Desired Feelings as a guide for living and working in line with your values. It takes a little time but is powerful work and is also an iterative process you can come back to.

5

IDENTIFYING YOUR BODY OF WORK AND RESOURCES BUILT OVER TIME

5.1 Your body of work over time

> *Your body of work is everything you create, contribute, affect, and impact. For individuals, it is the personal legacy you leave at the end of your life, including all the tangible and intangible things you have created. Individuals who structure their careers around autonomy, mastery, and purpose, will have a powerful body of work.*
>
> **Pamela Slim, *Body of Work*[44]**

In *Wholehearted,* we explore how the concept of looking at your body of work over time can be a very powerful framework and support for transition. It's valuable to invest in the effort to review your body of work values and ingredients. This is way more than a résumé, though that might be a useful starting point. And it's important to look at your whole life—volunteer and pro bono work as well as paid work. Working on body of work concepts with clients, I have noticed that work we do in a volunteer capacity can be underrated or dismissed but is actually a rich potential source of insight. Look too at how you operate in the world overall, for example the values we instil in our children or others around us and how we model or do this.

Here are the repeating and echoing themes in my life as expressed through my body of work:

- teaching and sharing my knowledge
- making a difference
- accentuating the positive, strengths and optimism
- leadership and self-leadership
- the value of solitude and quiet, introverted power
- creativity and innovation
- the power and wisdom of reading and writing
- knowing my personality as a tool for self-knowledge and growth.

You can see they are often overarching ingredients, an expression of what is valued and shaping a life and professional living with this central focus.

WHOLEHEARTED LIVING REFLECTIONS

What are the central themes in your life as expressed through your body of work? What are your key life and work ingredients that can provide a golden thread for your continuing journey?

5.2 Body of work and what it can tell us

In *Wholehearted* I take you through a few personal examples of projects, creative work and ideas I developed and led and the stream of threads running through them. This body of work provides a guide or bridge through times of transition.

WHOLEHEARTED LIVING REFLECTIONS

Have a look at one of the key threads or central themes you have identified in the previous section and see how it has played out over time in different ways.

_____
_____
_____
_____
_____

WHAT TO TAKE WITH YOU

When you are making a transition, identify what you don't want to leave behind. Keep taking your legacy and mission forward in new ways and building on it. These are valuable support processes and mechanisms that can propel you onwards, ones you are already invested in that reflect your values and passions. It might be skills you have developed over time like leadership, teaching, troubleshooting or caring for others that you can craft into new roles and ways of being. It can be easy to leave critical aspects of ourselves behind and undervalue them as we shift, so it's worth thinking about what you want to take forward and how.

Here are some areas I have reflected on as I have moved through transition and into life coaching, personality type work, tarot and making a difference in a new way via social media, online coaching and writing this book.

- How can leadership, for example, shed light on self-leadership?
- What have I learnt about self-leadership in my own leadership journey?
- How can I reframe or recast that to shed light on my direction?
- How can I make a difference in a new way?

WHOLEHEARTED LIVING REFLECTIONS

Working further with your key theme above, what questions might you ask yourself as a bridge to the future?

How can you take this aspect of your body of work forward in new ways?

5.3 Not leaving pieces of yourself behind

WHOLEHEARTED LIVING REFLECTIONS

Reflect further on these questions in thinking about taking yourself forward and not leaving important pieces behind.

What do you want to take with you and recast in new ways?

What do you want to leave behind and why?

What experiences of leaving have made you feel 'less than'?

How can you reframe them more positively now?

If it feels like a workplace or person doesn't value you any more, how can you value yourself as you move on?

How can body of work concepts help you not leave pieces of yourself behind?

_____

_____

_____

5.4 Turning points and leaving with grace

> *Research on transition and turning points has found that turning points are often single events and moments in time and transitions are an extended period rather than an event. The research also found that it is what we do at those critical turning points that makes a difference in our life narrative. Reflecting on those moments retrospectively also helps us see the coherence in our story.*[45]
>
> **Wholehearted: Self-leadership for Women in Transition**

Often there is a moment of knowing it is time to move on. But in there is also the pain of separation and feeling of loss even though we might wish to move on. With all of that, it's easy to overlook or forget our key strengths and leave them behind in the effort to shift.

There is also the opportunity to leave behind what is toxic, unhelpful or not what you want to be taking forward as part of your legacy and body of work in the world. Leaving with grace is possible at times. Other times we might find ourselves having to cut our losses and leave suddenly. What we do at those turning points and reflecting on this helps us make sense of our story.

This section of the *Wholehearted Companion Workbook* explores these aspects of turning point and change through looking at other women's experiences. I invite you to connect with these themes through the stories of women who share their heart and soul via *Wholehearted*

Stories on Quiet Writing. Reading the words of others and seeing what they stir up or connect to within you can be a powerful process for your own transition and navigation in a time of change. It provides an opportunity to explore such moments in your own life.

Women who have shared their *Wholehearted Stories* on Quiet Writing describe such moments of knowing it is time to move on. For some it has involved illness and a kind of breakdown or burnout—a physical feeling of being unable to return to the workplace or a situation that often means people don't return for a long time or ever. For others, it is a decisive moment that creates a turning point like the message delivered in the meeting that I experienced. I invite you to read these stories and experiences and reflect on your own situation or past experiences.

In *Breakdown to Breakthrough*[46] Lynn Hanford-Day talks about a 'heart attack of the soul':

> 'You're lucky. Some people have an actual heart attack, and some of them die' said a friend. His words really struck a chord in me. I may not have had a cardiac arrest yet I felt dead, lifeless, unable to function physically, psychologically, emotionally. My heart was still beating and that meant I was alive, apparently. I had flirted with burnout many times over previous years and had already read 'The Joy of Burnout' by Dina Glouberman three times. I had even done a retreat with her on the Greek island of Skyros for God's sake! But this was the big one. It is five years ago this January I woke up unable to move. I'd spent the previous three or four months feeling tired and by the time Christmas arrived, I felt utterly exhausted. I remember telling work colleagues I felt like I had run into a brick wall. I thought I needed a holiday and all would be well again. I never returned to my job as an HR Director, in fact, I didn't work for another 18 months.

Heidi Washburn, in *When the Inner Voice Calls, and Calls Again*, retells her moment:[47]

> *Back to the rainy fall night. As I said, I just wanted to get home to my bed. As I pulled onto the familiar Garden State Parkway, the rain let up and I relaxed. Before I could turn on the radio for entertainment a voice in my head came on instead. A quiet, gentle but firm voice, not just a thought.*
> *'I don't want to do this anymore.'*
> *What?*
> *'I said! I don't want to do this anymore.'*
> *What do you mean? You have to. You just got the business where you want it. You have staff, an office and now you can do the more creative work. Isn't that what you wanted? That was the end of the conversation. Or so I thought. After that night, after that very moment, everything changed but so quietly and slowly I hardly noticed. Of course, I was the one making the decisions. However, I didn't know where I was going or what the path was. Deep change doesn't come with a check-list or a schedule. And there is no guarantee that things will work out for the best.*

Katherine Bell talks in *Our Heart Always Knows the Way*[48] about the permission she felt to make a number of major changes all at once after reading David Whyte's *Crossing the Unknown Sea*:

> *With that first heart-leap of recognition, and the simple permission given by the Wonderful Mr Whyte, I took the plunge into the unknown sea towards work, life and relationship that was wholehearted. I tackled the problem in the only way I knew how to at the time, which was to leave my job, home, partner and city in the same week (not recommended) and take flight to the other side of the world for six weeks. My entire known life was in storage, ready to be dealt with when I got back.*

WHOLEHEARTED LIVING REFLECTIONS

What do these stories bring up for you about knowing when it is time to leave a situation, what to take and what to leave behind?

What do they suggest to you about leaving with grace when we can and when it might not be possible?

5.5 Resources for a new life

When shaping a new life, it is a wonderful time to reflect on the skills you already have and how to take them forward. Also to look at what skills you need to invest in to adapt and grow into a new version of you.

WHOLEHEARTED LIVING REFLECTIONS

So what resources do you have for a new life? Reflect on these questions as a compass to know what skills you want to invest time and money in to develop knowledge and wisdom.

What has intrigued you for the longest time that you haven't got around to?

What lights you up when you hear it mentioned?

What has recurred as a theme in your life over and over and especially at key points?

NEW SKILLS AND WAYS TO LEARN

New skills are like the foundation and the bricks of the building of you, piecing together your body of work and new ways of working. There are a myriad of ways to learn new skills and knowledge. Here's a quick list. You may be able to add others.

- Do a face-to-face course
- Seek out a mentor or coach
- Study online
- Gain qualifications or certification
- Read books that upskill and inspire you
- Invest a few moments each day in something that you love
- Learn via trial and error
- Find a buddy and learn together
- Go to a conference or event
- Follow people online
- Read blogs
- Read research papers
- Follow thought leaders in the area
- Listen to podcasts and audiobooks
- Practise through doing, like a master craftsperson
- Initiate creative projects and pieces
- Join associations or interest groups.

What are your personal learning preferences? For example studying alone, meeting others, learning online, getting a qualification, accreditation, deepening self-knowledge.

What are your learning goals now?

Why do you have these particular learning goals now?

Which ways of learning will help you best acquire the new skills you are seeking to grow?

How can you stretch in new ways?

Which transferable skills, knowledge and experience can support you as you move forward?

5.6 Finishing on a high note—closure, letting go and moving on

In *Wholehearted* I shared how I haven't always left situations well or finished on a high note. Often the desire to leave has trumped all, or other circumstances (such as caring for my mother) took over. I first wrote about finishing on a high note when I was leaving on a very low note—separated from my long-time workplace and dealing with redundancy after thirty-plus years of employment. Over time, I learnt to gain closure and leave with a sense of peace if not exactly how I would have planned!

WHOLEHEARTED LIVING REFLECTIONS

Whatever the circumstances, taking a moment to gain closure, let go and move on can help us shift positively. Identify the options most relevant to you and possible actions you can take for each of these prompts about finishing on a high note and feeling a sense of completion.

☐ 🐚 **Tie up the loose ends**

Where can you finish off any lingering or difficult tasks for an improved sense of completion?

....
....
....
....

☐ 🐚 **See things through to completion and celebrate that**

Where can you complete what is valuable and special, see it through in different ways and celebrate what you have done, let people know what you have achieved?

_____
_____
_____

☐ 🐚 **Say thank you**

How can you say thank you to someone—a family member, creator or someone you are leaving behind—whose work or life has impacted yours?

_____
_____
_____

☐ 🐚 **Forgive**

Who can you forgive? Realising that releasing the energy is so important in moving on.

_____
_____
_____

☐ 🐚 **Take what is valuable with you**

How can you take what you what is valuable, transferable and portable with you?

_____
_____
_____

CYCLES, ABANDONED SUCCESS AND THE EIGHT OF CUPS

> *And it's not just our work but our actual selves that we pour into what we do. Leaving it, admitting that the end result is no longer worth it, is very difficult.*[49]
>
> **Jessa Crispin,** *The Creative Tarot*

Take a moment to reflect further on the Eight of Cups tarot card, abandoned success and choosing to walk away from the future you imagined. Transition is about identity and moving on. It often means leaving behind an identity we invested ourselves in. This can feel sad or disappointing, like we have erred, and we can give ourselves a hard time in the wake of this.

WHOLEHEARTED LIVING REFLECTIONS

To help you start a new beginning in a more unencumbered way, reflect on this identity you have invested yourself in and what it means to be leaving it behind.

How might you honour that identity in a meaningful way as you move on?

Thinking of the Eight of Cups tarot card, which are the full and useful cups in your life? What would you like to leave behind? Which are the empty cups best not carried forward?

5.7 Job-seeking, promotions, creative opportunities

In *Wholehearted* I share insights based on my experiences about how we might respond when events don't turn out as we planned in the area of job-seeking, promotions and creative opportunities. It is so easy to get into a cycle of damning self-worth. But you know what? I realised way later that those jobs I didn't get were actually the best thing that happened to me. Even though I felt quite damaged by the process at the time, in hindsight I can see how they simply were not the path for me.

WHOLEHEARTED LIVING REFLECTIONS

Take a moment to reflect on the job you didn't get, the promotion you were not chosen for, the creative opportunity that didn't go your way or even the person you desired who was not for you.

How did it make you feel?

What did you tell yourself about that?

How can you recast that narrative and see it differently?

How can you value yourself in moments like this when loss feels so prevalent?

5.8 Reframing redundancy, being 'deleted' and obsolescence

A classic time when our sense of personal worth and value is tested is when we are made redundant, our job is 'deleted' and we are 'obsolete'. Just read those words and see how they make us feel! They ring of shame and a challenge to our identity.

You might be a person dealing with people going through such experiences. Or you might be going through or have gone through one or more such experiences yourself. Perhaps you have been impacted by redundancy in your family, feeling the hurt and disappointment of others. In the context of the covid pandemic, so many have been impacted for reasons well beyond their control.

People respond differently, and circumstances, length of service and how invested we have been will impact on the feelings. I know from my own experience that even though I desperately wanted and needed to move on, it still hurt, especially in how the situation was managed. And that feeling of damage, loss of belonging and something like shame can reverberate for a long time.

WHOLEHEARTED LIVING REFLECTIONS

How can you take inspiration from the Holden story and Ashley Winnett's view that it was not the worker's fault to reframe redundancy or loss in a new way for yourself and others?

How can you shift to a new paradigm of reframing your personal worth whatever the circumstances?

5.9 Investing in our wisdom, crafting our journey and building our cathedral

If we think of each day as work on the cathedral of our creative life journey, it feels like we are working towards something larger and more significant: a book, a body of work, a series, a portfolio career, a self-sustaining creative business, a skill set we can be proud of and products and services we can share that spring from the rich soil of all the time we have invested.

Wholehearted: Self-leadership for Women in Transition

WHOLEHEARTED LIVING REFLECTIONS

What's the bigger picture, the cathedral you are building in your creative life journey?

_____
_____
_____
_____
_____

Where might you choose to invest in your wisdom and skill as a bridge to a new life?

_____
_____
_____
_____
_____

What have you always wanted to do?

How can you put the next steps in place?

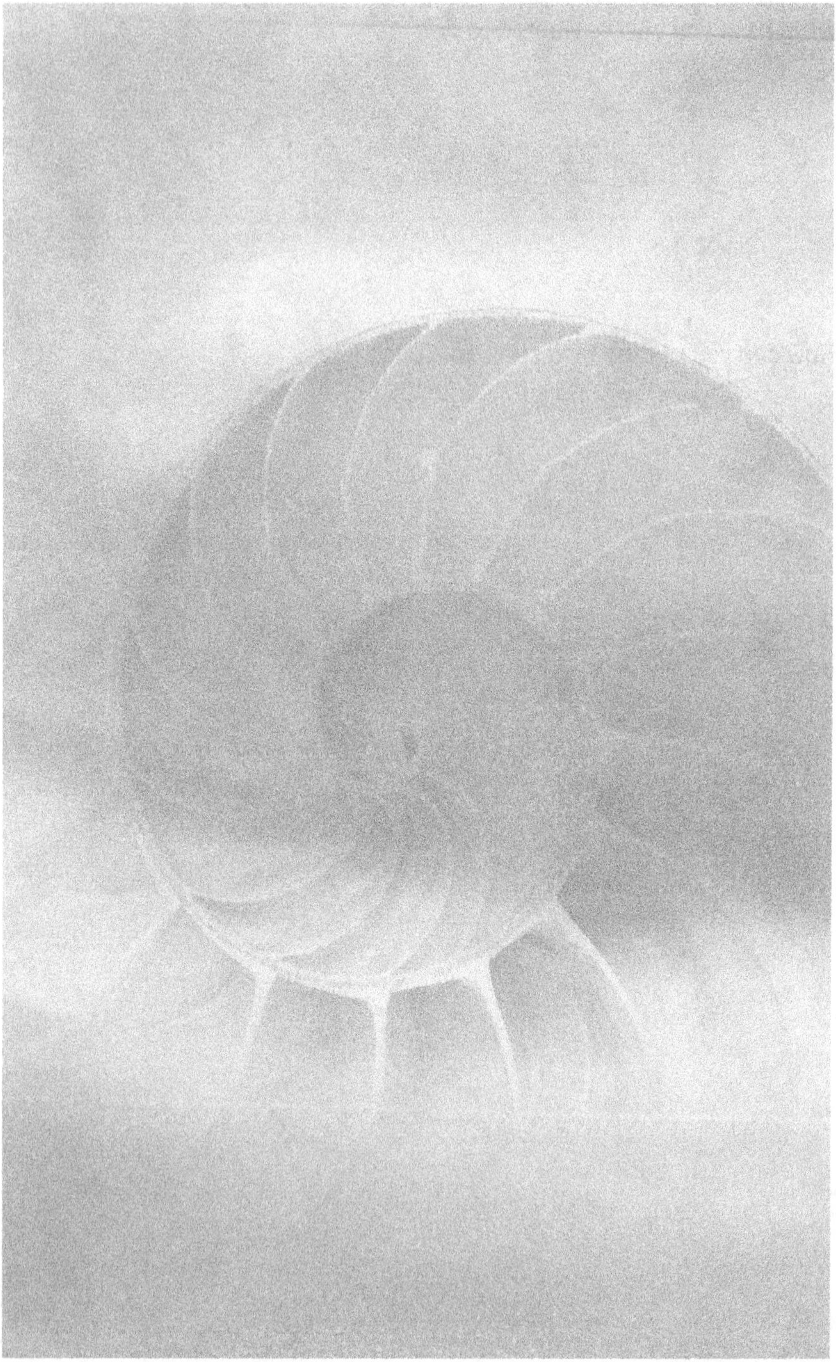

PART TWO

WHOLEHEARTED SELF-LEADERSHIP SKILLS

6

WHOLEHEARTED SELF-LEADERSHIP SKILLS

6.1 Setting powerful heartfelt intentions

In *Wholehearted* I share my experiences with setting powerful intentions from the heart in a deep way to make real change in my life. Specifically I charted my intention, setting course over time via the Softly Wild course at the turning point phase of my transition journey.

Here is more on this journey with further detail from my field journals to illustrate the process. It shows how working with intentions in an iterative way over time can yield results that go way beyond the surface level.

In the third time on the journey, I wrote in the front of my field notebook:

This is my third time on this journey. Each time is a bit like being a different butterfly. New ventures, new journeys, new realisations. They have been like landmarks on my journey, lighthouses, stakes in shifting sand and if not for them, I would not be where I am now. The first time was when I was in Wagga two years ago now. The images are all of wanting to be home, a sea change, being at home, setting up my office at home, reading space and space for books, writing and there were images of peacocks, swans, hummingbirds. I embraced so much spirit and overcame so much resistance. I dedicated the journal and time to the pursuit of quietness and the search for a lifestyle that has quietness at its core. And the book captures all the opening up around that—the podcasts, the books, the coaching, the birth of quiet writing as a concept.

My intention for that first time was:

> *I intend to be receptive to Softly Wild and work through all resistance to connect to a new intuitive way.*

I knew I was feeling resistance in so many ways and it was vital to break through these layers to craft a new life.

The second time through was harder but the field notebook foreshadowed a time of hunkering down at home, stillness within and finding sanctuary. It also foreshadowed books as the heart of things and intuition connecting thought and feeling as key. Embracing the ocean was a strong theme as well as writing, my core desired feelings and the Queen of Swords.

My intention at that time was:

> *I intend to intuitively connect thought and feeling to craft a new way to live through quiet writing.*

And the field book dedication:

> *I dedicate this notebook to making the connection between head and heart.*

The quote that sat at the front of my field book amid the images selected was by Hermann Hesse:

> *Within you, there is a stillness and a sanctuary to which you can retreat at any time and be yourself.*

This became a time of deep connection between head and heart and crafting a new way of life through quiet writing as a way of living and a business to be in the most practical of ways.

The third time around and a few months later into this journey and it meant all that and more: swimming with fish, embracing the ocean fully not just walking on the shore, getting among it, getting into creativity too—writing deeply, carving that softly wild life from pen, paper, what's in my head. It meant grounding myself in words, tarot, oracle, salt baths, bushwalks, keys of a keyboard I play like a piano as I listen to gentle music as my muse, feet on the floor.

It became a time of centring, calm creativity, walking a road, swimming a straight line, rising up, clear as a bell, fresh, connected, allowing myself to be creative, no longer misdirecting the energy elsewhere.

My intention for this field notebook and stage of the journey was:

> *I intend to calmly bring together my creative passions to be wholehearted and clear, inspiring others to be the same.*

Completing the passage from the woman who was lost to one who feels wholehearted, it was also about my impact and how I can inspire others to do the same. The quote chosen at the time in the front of my field notebook is from Virginia Woolf:

> *Odd how the creative power at once brings the whole universe into order.*

Working with intentions starts from the present moment but can be a rich iterative and spiralling upward journey as we learn new things over time, repeating lessons on another level. But if not for the intention setting in the first place, we would not be there at all.

WHOLEHEARTED LIVING REFLECTIONS

Here are some reflection questions for you on intention setting in your life.

How are you using the power of intention setting in the day-to-day now?

_____

_____

_____

How could you set your intentions in deeper ways you can track and build on over time?

_____

_____

_____

What resonates from my learning and transition that you could explore and apply in your own life?

_____

_____

_____

CONNECTING OUR INTENTIONAL PRACTICES

We can also supercharge our intentional practices by linking them up. Often we will find we have started a number of personal practices as we move into a time of transition but often they are disconnected. Some ways that I have integrated intentional approaches is through consciously looking at the connections between my key passions and practices. Once we connect up our intentions and ways of working with them, stronger self-leadership and self-awareness emerges. At a time of transition, these are two areas you want to be growing and tapping into for inner wisdom on an ongoing basis.

For example, I gained pace and strength with my intentional way of working and self-leadership when I connected up Morning Pages with tarot, astrology and moon cycle work. The linkages emerged over time, coming from my daily practices.

I started to keep track of the lunar cycles more as I wrote in my Morning Pages. At the new moon, I work with a tarot spread to help me connect with my intuitive and symbolic wisdom. Through reading astrology reports, I understood the energies of each particular moon cycle and its opportunities. In detail, I work through the tarot spread and its messages, documenting my journey in a notebook and writing the story of guidance for the cycle to come. From this process, I set an intention for the lunar cycle.

As an example, my current one as I am writing is:

> *I quiet my mind and rest. I am the queen of my thoughts. I am clear and wise and able to share and lead with my own voice.*

These words were distilled from a six-card tarot reading in the context of my life and the lunar and astrological conditions of the time. Each day, I read this intention and honour it first thing as part of my Morning Pages practice. I have the cycles of the moon in front of me and I see where I am in the cycle: setting and feeling my intention; trusting it and relaxing into it; and when it's a time of receiving and giving back. I can course-correct, feel it come into being or navigate another way. As Ezzie Spencer reminds in *Lunar Abundance*,[50] the beauty of working with lunar cycles is that we have an opportunity to start afresh with each new moon with our intentions.

Here are some tips for connecting intentional practices for deeper and more sustained self-leadership:

- Identify the practices you are already doing or want to start to do to build more intention into your daily life.
- Look at the natural connections between these systems or practices.

- See how you can make practical and concrete links, for example connecting your intention across your journalling and yoga practices.
- Use visual prompts and different ways to remind yourself of your intentions, such as signage around you, on your screensavers, via your planning system, in your journal.

WHOLEHEARTED LIVING REFLECTIONS

What intentional practices do you engage in now or are you interested in developing further?

How can you truly be more intentional rather just writing words and not anchoring into them as you move through life?

How can you connect intention setting for deeper value and in visual ways building on the natural cycles and activities of your life?

6.2 Writing as daily practice

Writing as daily or regular practice is a cornerstone of positive transition and self-leadership insights. Here I share more detailed suggestions and strategies for daily writing practice and how to make it work for you. I also suggest ways in which regular writing practice can help connect our passions and structure our writing projects to achieve real desired outcomes.

DAILY WRITING PRACTICE AND HOW TO MAKE IT WORK FOR YOU

One of the things that makes a regular writing practice harder than it needs to be is having strict notions of what it must look like; for example I must write by hand, I must finish this journal, I must write three pages each day, the notebook must be beautiful, I only write in the evenings. Instead of being hard and fast about it and having too many expectations, find the approach and method that works for you to get the writing done. Even though practices like Morning Pages are simple, we can easily overcomplicate them or not do them in a way that works for us.

In *Wholehearted* I shared the story of Ellen Bard and how she writes regularly via Morning Pages and advocates that there is no 'one size fits all' approach. Here is a little more from *The Creative Penn* podcast interview to consider:

> *I think there's a few different things for 'Morning Pages', and I think you can use it in different ways as well. I think that's important. One thing, for example, is I do my 'Morning Pages' on the computer. So I have some chronic pain issues, and free-writing for me is not very fun. I don't enjoy it. It hurts. So, I would much rather type. And actually, I find that the words actually flow onto the page more easily.*

Julia Cameron, who wrote 'The Artist's Way,' I feel she wanted people to free-write because it was 20 years ago, and we didn't have computers. And so before, people like you and I were so fluid with our computers, that we just don't think about typing. I think we can be flexible about 'Morning Pages'. So I type mine out. I think you can do several things. Free-writing is literally just writing whatever's in your head. And I think that can be really useful for, just like cleaning out. Imagine you're sweeping a house, that's what I think of. Get rid of whatever stuff is mumbling along in your head, whatever you're thinking about. Just get it out on the page, clean it out. And then, if you want to later you can go back and see was there anything useful in that.

But journaling is a practice, and I think you can use 'Morning Pages' as a way of journaling as well, can be super helpful for people who are trying to process something difficult. I think the research suggests something like 3 to 5 sessions of maybe 15 to 20 minutes each, on one particular issue. And that's enough to I guess process it, and de-charge it for people. Take out some of the heightened notions around it. And that's an incredibly powerful practice.[51]

WHOLEHEARTED LIVING REFLECTIONS

Do you have a regular writing practice now? If so, how is it going? If not, why not?

_____

_____

What are some of your natural preferences or 'heightened notions' around regular writing or Morning Pages?

_____

_____

How can you make a regular writing practice work better for you? Think: time of day, method of writing, notebook, how long, purpose, where you write.

Read Penelope Love's *Wholehearted Stories* contribution, 'The Journey to Write Here',[52] and jot down any inspiring thoughts from Penelope's engagement with Morning Pages and writing practice over the long term.

ANY WRITING WILL DO: HOW TO EMBED DAILY WRITING IN YOUR LIFE VIA PROJECTS AND PRACTICES

I encourage regular writing such as via Morning Pages as a fundamental self-anchoring practice, but I also encourage you to see how daily writing can be embedded into your life as much as possible.

An example of how this has happened for me has been my *Tarot Narrative* work. I never set out to do a tarot reading each day and share it on Instagram but that is exactly what happened. It has been a central part of my transition journey and I cannot imagine a day without getting up, doing my Morning Pages, then settling into my intuition with a three-card combined tarot and oracle reading, reading about it and working through the insights and wisdom and then writing a Tarot Narrative or story for the day.

At the heart of my transition journey, I worked intensively on this combined tarot and writing practice, posting full narratives on Instagram every day. I wrote the pieces in Notes on my computer so they were easy to copy, paste, update and keep as a running record. To make sure this happened each day, I taught myself to do it in parts if need be. But I got that intuitive work and the writing practice around it done each day without fail for six months.

I copied the files into Scrivener as a monthly Tarot Narrative and surprise, the file for each month is around 7,000 words. So over five months, with this daily practice focus and a commitment to showing up, I wrote 42,000 words. I have since streamlined this practice into a daily Instagram Stories distilled Tarot Narrative reading. But this period of intense intuitive work and writing practice helped me to shape and integrate both writing and intuition into my life.

The big message in this is: find a writing project that ignites your heart and passion and work on it daily or at least regularly. Break it into manageable and meaningful chunks somehow, and especially if your goal is a creative and writing-focused one, write each day or regularly.

I wrote the first draft of this book as part of NaNoWriMo[53] (National Novel Writing Month) and I committed to writing 1,667 words each day and 50,000 words in total for the month of November 2017. It might be hard to keep up a process like this each day, but you never know until you try and experience the feelings it inspires. You can also adapt these principles into something more sustainable or manageable for you like 500 words a day. That becomes 10,000 words a month if you just write on weekdays, which is a significant body of writing!

Suddenly daily writing practice is a source of so much knowledge, insight, inspiration and productivity that you will wonder why you never started it before. The keyboard feels like a piano you are playing, the words come and with it, your life in transition is suddenly a book you are writing, a memoir, or a structure that makes sense instead of a rambling thing you cannot quite pin down.

WHOLEHEARTED LIVING REFLECTIONS

List some ways you can embed writing into your daily life.

_____
_____
_____

What writing project would you love to shape and how might it be structured or achieved in small steps?

_____
_____

Share your regular writing strategies and projects on social media with the hashtag #selfleadershipbook

6.3 Practising mindfulness

> *Something happens when you dive into a world where clocks don't tick and inboxes don't ping. As your arms circle, swing and pull along the edge of a vast ocean, your mind wanders, and you open yourself to awe, to the experience of seeing something astonishing, unfathomable or greater than yourself.*
>
> **Julia Baird, *Phosphorescence*[54]**

I loved reading Sydney author Julia Baird's recent book *Phosphorescence* and especially how she celebrates her joy of ocean swimming. Of all the mindful practices I have worked on in my transition time, swimming has been perhaps the strongest anchor. This is the time I've been able to let go, feel peace, settle and as Julia Baird describes soak myself in a sense of wonder, awe and being part of something immense. It puts things in perspective and solutions arrive as if by magic rather than analytic thought. I shared my thoughts on swimming in a piece on Quiet Writing—'10 amazing life lessons from swimming in the sea'.[55]

The key ingredient is mindfulness, being purely in the moment. I share with you in *Wholehearted* how accessing a meditative state for me is through everyday activities like this: walking, yoga, writing, tarot. And this is personal. Each of us needs to find our own way. For you it might be cooking, doing jigsaw puzzles, climbing a mountain, colouring in, painting or meditating.

Your personality preferences are a key factor here too. Swimming helps me balance because it helps me get out of my head and into a sensing mode. Building what you need more of into your life can help psychologically with being grounded. Introverts might need to get outside and activate their senses more. Extraverts might need to learn to go within and seek ways to activate a still centre of calm alone.

Remember too Kethledge and Erwin's important book *Lead Yourself First*,[56] which explores all kinds of practices for self-leadership which often involve increased mindfulness. They can be physical activities such as bricklaying and running, or analytical ones such as list-building.

WHOLEHEARTED LIVING REFLECTIONS

What practices help you to be truly mindful and in the moment?

What might you need more of from a personality perspective for balance?

How might you explore new ways of finding this stillness and sense of being in the moment?

What is one thing you will try this week?

6.4 Visioning and strategy skills

In *Wholehearted*, I share examples of how I identified and nurtured my ability to create a vision for my new life and the strategic skills to make it happen. Everyone is different in how they will do this. It is a stronger preference for some than others, but we can all do this in our own way. Your way might be more visual than verbal; it might be a mind-map rather than a list. Or you might mix up your approaches.

This is an opportunity to identify your personal examples and styles of envisioning and strategising and ways to build on them.

WHOLEHEARTED LIVING REFLECTIONS

First of all, how would you rate your ability to create a vision and make a strategy? Give yourself a score out of ten.

How do you feel about your strategy and vision skills?

Where have you used them in your life to great effect, drawing on the more holistic and intuitive to craft the future or options? Think of an example and write down what worked.

What is your personal style of visioning and strategising? How do you prefer to do this? Alone, in a group, listing, mind-mapping, writing a mission statement, based on values, gathering information over time, using something visual and practical you can have in front of you, using colour, digitally, by hand, journalling.

How might you use your personal style of visioning and strategy skills now and into the future—near or far—to help your transition journey and to achieve your heart's desires?

6.5 Understanding your personality and unique gifts

In *Wholehearted* I share the journey of understanding my preference for Introverted Intuiting and how I have learnt to work with its special gifts. Each personality type has its own unique gifts and preferences.

Here, I take you on a deeper journey into my own gift of Introverted Intuiting as an example, explain more about the layers and insights psychological type can offer you as a form of self-leadership. This builds on the insights and information in 4.2 and 4.3.

UNDERSTANDING MY GIFTS AND STRENGTHS OF INTROVERTED INTUITING

I have worked through my personality and psychological type over time to understand myself. Learning more about my natural preferences provided great insight. In particular, knowing the strength of my introversion and how I needed to care and honour my introvert made all the difference in my life.

Reading Susan Cain's book *Quiet* helped me understand how the way I felt about my introversion was a consequence of being in a society where the Extravert Ideal dominates. It has been easy to feel like a square peg in a round hole, even though there are a lot of square peg introverts just like me—about 40 per cent of the population.

With the support of evidence and facts, I was able to see more deeply that as an introvert, I need quiet to recharge and I like to interact with the world through the support and lens of time alone. I learnt that I needed to see this as something to honour—to learn to close the door, to seek solitude as a core part of my day and source of creativity and to manage my energy through working my introversion as a strength not a weakness.

Whether it was reading books, writing, working with tarot, walking on the beach, or swimming, all of these activities helped me gather my thoughts and operate more successfully. As *Lead Yourself First*[57] shows, we need to lead ourselves before we are able to effectively lead others and to do that we need to know ourselves. We need to do those activities that help us to connect the pieces, honour the energy of silence and of clarifying thought and accessing our intuition.

For extraverts, the journey to honour will be a different one, one more focused on the need for energy via people, variety, interaction, networks and social connections. But as Michael S Erwin, an extravert and co-author of *Lead Yourself First*, found, self-leadership through solitude is an important practice for extraverts as well.

Learning how to access my intuition and listen to it and work it as part of my introverted nature has been key in my transition journey. I had to learn new skills and to apply old skills in new ways to connect with my Introverted Intuiting to enable it to guide me through this time.

Restarting Morning Pages and starting daily Tarot Narrative practice were critical to knowing how my Introverted Intuiting works as a strength. These practices tap into my inner intuitive compass so I can navigate through times of change.

UNDERSTANDING YOUR GIFTS AND STRENGTHS

That is a key part of my 'gift differing' and you will have yours. It might be Introverted Feeling, connected with internal values or Introverted Sensing connected with sensory memory and seeing the detail of encounters over time like a movie reel in your head you can access as a resource. Or it might be Extraverted Intuiting and exploring possibilities of a situation far into the future, combining unique elements into something only you can see.

Understanding the gift of how you are wired, your preferred cognitive ways of working, is an important step in the journey of being wholehearted. You might find that what makes you feel oversensitive, vulnerable and overly empathic can also help you to heal others and support others in their changes in fundamental ways. You might find your empathic ability makes you an excellent intuitive or channeller for others, or a writer who can create emotion or find a structure to help others with their own emotional states of being.

Knowing your strengths also helps you to be able to deploy them effectively. It is as if we have a responsibility as part of wholehearted living to know our tools, our gifts, our calling, our secret ingredients. To bring them out into the sunshine and polish them up like a secret stone or unearthed fossil in some cases, to see what the colours and textures really are.

Introverted or Extraverted, Intuitive or Sensing, Thinking or Judging, Feeling or Perceiving and the unique combination of these in our cognitive skill set gives us an armoury of skills and strengths. But we need to understand them, articulate them and learn to see them as strengths and unique gifts not weaknesses or something that holds us back, just because it feels different.

It is a way of deep diving into yourself as well. Identifying and knowing your preferences is a way in. Once you start working through that, it is a multi-layered and deep resource for understanding yourself.

WHOLEHEARTED LIVING REFLECTIONS

Look at the table below of cognitive functions, gifts and keywords and descriptions drawn from the work of Carl Jung, Mary McGuiness, James Graham Johnston, Nicole Gruel, Susan Nash and Sue Blair. This is an introduction to the rich world of cognitive gifts based on how we are wired. We use all the functions but some are more natural and our zone of genius than others.

Cognitive functions (Carl Jung/Mary McGuiness)[58]	Transcendent dimensions/Gift's Compass™(James Graham Johnston[59] and Nicole Gruel)[60]	Keywords drawn from McGuiness, Johnston–Gruel and *The Type Trilogy* by Susan Nash and Sue Blair[61]
Extraverted Sensing— Sensory experience	The Realistic Gift	Engaging the senses, gathering from what is present, experiencing, observing, focusing
Introverted Sensing —Sensory memory	The Aesthetic Gift	Subjective impressions, known from experience, recalling, comparing
Extraverted Intuition— Exploring possibilities	The Catalytic Gift	What's possible, new, potential, innovation, scanning, exploring, brainstorming
Introverted Intuition— Visionary insight	The Visionary Gift	Working with the unseen, symbolism, making meaning, inner vision, insight
Extraverted Thinking— Logical outcomes	The Constructive Gift	Working with external facts, practical order, organising, logical solutions, structure
Introverted Thinking— Internal analysis	The Conceptual Gift	Clear, logical independent thought, complex reasoning, reframing, critiquing
Extraverted Feeling— Harmonizing people	The Social Gift	Empathy, tuning in to others, harmonising, consensus, nurturing, addressing concerns
Introverted Feeling— Universal values	The Idealistic Gift	Tuning into and living by personal values, interconnection, ethics, valuing difference

See which one or two of the eight cognitive functions resonate with you the most as your potential gifts. Make a note of this and reflect on this gift and what it might mean for you and your transition and work in the world and for others.

LAYERS OF PERSONALITY STRENGTHS AND KNOWLEDGE: DIFFERENT LENSES AND WORKING WITH A COACH

To really know your personality better, it is ideal to work through it with a coach to unlock the potential of this insight, so you can gain knowledge and a framework for making sense of yourself and how you operate in interaction with others.

You will gain access to knowledge about your preferred cognitive functions—your Dominant, Auxiliary, Tertiary and Inferior cognitive functions such as Introverted Intuiting or Extraverted Feeling—and how the other functions might play out as well in different ways in your personality. From this, you can know your gift, your auxiliary or supporting function, your tertiary function and your inferior function.

This eight-function model gives a powerful framework for personality and consciousness. It can help us leverage our strengths, harness our less preferred areas and balance ourselves by working with our opposites. Working with a coach trained in psychological type frameworks can help you to understand your personality and how it might naturally work in a deeper way.

Another lens of personality you might work through is Temperament. Based on the work of David Keirsey,[62] the four-letter personality types can also be grouped into four temperament groups as follows:

Artisans (SP): ESTP, ISTP, ESFP, ISFP
Guardians (SJ): ESTJ, ISTJ, ESFJ, ISFJ
Idealists (NF): ENFJ, INFJ, ENFP, INFP
Rationals (NT): ENTJ, INTJ, ENTP, INTP

Each of these temperaments is a unique and easily recognisable configuration of character traits that we can use to understand ourselves and others. Focusing on the factors that distinguish the temperaments and personality styles from each other, Temperament theory is very useful as a framework for understanding and respecting difference.

There are so many lenses through which we can look at personality. Once you have this knowledge, you can link it up with other tools and systems.

I like to see how the sixteen personality types line up with tarot. There are sixteen court cards in tarot as well and there is a link between the four tarot elements, personality type and the court cards that I find especially useful from both the angle of personality and the view of tarot reading, working both ways in and out of each system.

Once you enter the world of personality self-knowledge, you will wonder how you ever managed without its insights into our strengths and gifts, as well as its value for understanding the gifts of others. It is all about understanding the self as a unique entity of gifts and opportunities so we can work our personality to the best of its potential and understand and be respectful of the differences of others.

You can also work with me on finding out about your personality type and its gifts via Personality Stories Coaching and ecourses.[63]

WHOLEHEARTED LIVING REFLECTIONS

Write down any questions you might have about understanding your personality, unique gifts and strengths.

Identify ways to seek answers, for example reading, coaching, journalling, mentoring, conferences, professional development.

6.6 Getting the work done (practical execution)

In *Wholehearted*, I share three key strategies for getting the work done:

1. Show up for yourself
2. Show up for your ideas
3. Working with others

Here I take you deeper into examples and strategies for practical execution.

1. Show up for yourself

Showing up for yourself is about the creative and project work that is important to you but also about ways you support yourself via self-care and connection so you feel energised, self-nourished and able to create.

I recommend trying Charlie Gilkey's Time Blocking technique and tools as a practical framework for scheduling activity in four different kinds of blocks: Focus, Admin, Social and Recovery Blocks.[64] The Time Blocking tool helps you organise your week in blocks by activity type. My clients and I have experienced success and increased productivity with this approach. Simply working out where everything goes helps you make time for your priorities and to show up for them, just as you would for any other appointment.

WHOLEHEARTED LIVING REFLECTIONS

How can you better schedule time for yourself and your priorities and show up and not let yourself down? Jot down your thoughts on this.

What is super important to you—like writing or other creative work or self-care—that is not getting prioritised?

Think of the best time too for what matters, such as writing or walking first thing in the morning to make sure it gets done. What time of the day works best for what matters in your life?

2. Show up for your ideas

I shared a case study of working on writing, getting the initial ideas and shaping the beginning of *Wholehearted* via NaNoWriMo and showing up to my ideas to bring them into a more concrete form. Here are some other ideas and options for practical creative productivity and capturing ideas in more detail. And some prompts for you to do the same.

CAPTURE IDEAS AND PRACTICAL WAYS TO TAKE THEM FORWARD

The first step in converting your inspiration into action and outcomes is to capture those inspiring ideas so they are not lost. They can come in all manner of ways and situations, so you need to be ready.

I have some of my best ideas in the shower and in the middle of the night, often in dreams and semi-awake moments. You think, 'I'll remember later, when I wake in the morning.' The reality is that you often don't, and it is critical to capture your ideas as an initial step on the path to strategy, execution and outcomes.

Make sure you have a physical notebook or an electronic system for capturing ideas. Digital options include Things App, Evernote and Trello. Do whatever works for you but having a personal system for capturing ideas is a fundamental step to pinning them down.

Evernote is fabulous for capturing resources and your ideas about them in one place. The great thing about Evernote is that you can tag each article or link with hashtags on a particular topic so you can find them later. I use Evernote to draft my notes on articles, resources, courses and ecourses. You can save them over time so you can easily go back to them to pick up on ideas and take them forward or share them.

The best way forward is to find a way to structure your thoughts into something deliverable: an outline for a book, a plan for an ecourse, the flow of a blog post, the pieces of a puzzle, the theme of an artwork, a mission statement or a project framework.

That is where all your captured notes come in. See how you can structure them into a form that is easier to work with such as:

- a draft blog post structure in your journal, Scrivener, Word or directly into your blogging platform
- a book outline in a notebook, via sticky notes, Scrivener or Trello where you can start to shape and shift around chapters or themes
- an implementation plan for a larger project like a new business, website or ecourse idea, chunking it into achievable steps you can track and make happen.

You may be more free-flowing and not want too much structure. That is fine but at least have an idea of your intention, where you want to head, what you want to create and how you can practically make this happen.

As EL Doctorow says:

> *It's like driving a car at night. You never see further than your headlights, but you can make the whole trip that way.*[65]

Showing up is a matter of will, intention and preparation, and the three working together can work magic. Working out how you are going to get there with your outline, digital notes, timeline or project plan helps build a bridge to make it happen. And then you show up to your ideas: each morning, to write and work; to complete the self-learning goals you set for yourself; to make the plan to change your life into the positive state you desire.

So I encourage you to create the map of your success and vision. Work out what that larger direction looks like so you can step yourself through it day by day, piece by piece.

WHOLEHEARTED LIVING REFLECTIONS

How can you capture your ideas and work out ways to take them forward practically? Jot down your thoughts on this—how you do it now and what else might work for you.

What is your intention or vision for the creative project or transition that is important to you?

How can you capture ideas and put them into a container or structure so you can work with them?

How do you then take your ideas forward into an executable plan? Once you've identified them, how do you work out what you want to do with them to get forward action and a return on investment? For example, create an ecourse or resource, write a book, plan a business.

What will help you show up to your ideas day by day, week by week to shape what you desire?

3. Working with others

In *Wholehearted*, I share the story of Hayley Carr, from a conversation on *The Art of Creative Living* podcast[66] with Nicola Newman as an example of complementary partnership. We can build skills ourselves but we can also work with others whose skills balance ours.

Those skills might be ones that are not within our natural preferences, skills that we are not interested in developing. Or they may be an area we want to grow within ourselves. For example, I worked with editor Penelope Love on the early drafts of *Wholehearted* to get assistance and to learn. I have written much over time but have not previously shaped a book-length manuscript into something more manageable and readable. I realised this step of the process was less in line with my skills and I needed the balance. Penelope helped me with developmental editing and looking at the book shape and flow as a whole with all her years of experience in editing and publishing. And that made all the difference. This continues to be an important partnership for me personally and as an independent author. Even though we might desire to be independent in authorship and other ways, partnerships can help us achieve our goals.

Knowing our strengths helps us identify when we are working in our zone of genius and when we need to learn and extend our skills or seek assistance. Working with others is a time-efficient and supportive way to work and grow. You can keep it small and focused, as Paul Jarvis demonstrates in his book *Company of One*,[67] framed on your zone of specialty, working out what matters, not going too big and seeking specialists that work in a small team with you to achieve results. Or it might be choosing the right coach or accountability partner. It all helps in the practical execution and getting things done.

WHOLEHEARTED LIVING REFLECTIONS

In what areas of your life would you benefit from some balance and assistance, a leg up?

_____

_____

_____

Who might help you as a partner with the right skills and preferences to complement you and get things done?

_____
_____
_____

Who might you partner with to learn new skills?

_____
_____
_____

Getting the work done and practical execution is also a central focus in Sacred Creative Collective Group Coaching, so if you'd like the support of a group and a coach in shaping, completing and finishing a creative project or transition, that might be a powerful option for you.[68]

6.7 Building connection and community

We all need wholehearted support and community for creativity and transition. As we go through times of change and shift from workplaces or locations, we can find this is a time to build on our existing connections in different ways. In *Wholehearted* I shared my experience of this and how my world is now a much richer place especially through the power of online connections and community.

I encourage you to open your heart to like-minded women in this way too. Here I share three practical strategies for building community, support and connection to support you in times of transition.

1. Social media connection and hashtag challenges

The main way I built my online community and connection is via showing up regularly on social media and connecting with other women. Connecting via hashtag challenges is a central part of this. I am not even sure how some of us connected initially, but we are firm friends via sharing our lives online, photos of the day-to-day, our progress and celebrations and our sadness and frustrations.

Top tip: Connect with kindred others online via engaging with hashtags and challenges.

Connect with people in your sphere of interest: writing, tarot, art, creativity, midlife, ageing positively, travel, whatever it might be, via hashtags. Seek out opportunities to grow your connections via these kindred interests through online hashtag challenges.

The host of the challenge selects a time period—a month, a week, a year—and tailors prompts to engage and connect. People share a photo and thoughts about the prompt and hashtag for and through that can find others who might also share interests. Susannah Conway[69] has some brilliant community challenges during the year, mostly on Instagram but also on Facebook. And there are challenges every day of the week encouraging you to notice, dig deep, create, learn and connect with like-minded others. Check out these hashtags for ideas and connection: #decemberreflections2020 (and every year) #taleswithfriends #readingwomenchallenge

WHOLEHEARTED LIVING REFLECTIONS

What areas of interest and hashtags would be a possible connection point on social media?

_____
_____
_____
_____

Research and note down some upcoming challenges to try out and connect with others.

_____
_____
_____
_____

Commit to one you will do in the near future and aim to show up regularly. Or create your own!

_____
_____
_____
_____

2. Connecting via online course and group coaching communities

Another key point of connection and community for me has been through online and group coaching programs and communities. You might notice in *Wholehearted* how many of my connections are from engaging with group courses and coaching online as I have built new skills and sought out new ways of living and working. And now I lead my own group coaching communities to support others in the wisdom of connected online learning.

Top tip: Combine learning with group interactions.

One-to-one coaching provides a personal deep dive but group coaching and learning has the advantage of collective wisdom and learning from others. Through learning and making progress together, we often make deep connections that can take us forward in new ways. Plus it's fabulous accountability support for getting on with what is important.

WHOLEHEARTED LIVING REFLECTIONS

What learning priorities do you have and how might connecting with a group learning or coaching community help with this?

_____
_____
_____
_____

Identify some options for you for group learning or coaching.

_____
_____
_____
_____

What might you create as a group learning, coaching or accountability offering to foster connection and community?

_____
_____
_____
_____

3. From online to meeting in person

Another key step for me was making sure I made time to connect with people I met online in other ways. It might be saying, 'How about we hop on and have a Zoom chat?' or making plans to meet in person. When travelling, you might integrate times and locations to meet special online connections in person. And look for opportunities to take those online connections a little further.

You never know where that might lead. It can feel strange at first but often you know each other very well from connecting via social media and meeting one to one whether digitally or in person can be a fabulous experience.

Top tip: Don't be afraid to reach out to others where you feel a connection and meet one-to-one digitally or in person.

Here are some examples from my life:

- Online friend Beth Cregan invited me via Instagram to join her in writing at dawn each day after I commented on a post about this. It's become the backbone of my writing routine and practice.
- I reached out to Instagram connection Penelope Love to help me with my *Wholehearted* book because I wasn't sure of the next steps and felt stuck. This became a beautiful editing partnership that enabled my book draft to come into being as two books and a friendship I am deeply appreciative of.
- I have connected with a number of online friends from Instagram and courses in cafes and pubs in Manchester, London, Vienna, Frankfurt, Glastonbury and other places and had the best heart-to-heart connections.

WHOLEHEARTED LIVING REFLECTIONS

Who might you reach out to for deeper connection, learning and accountability from your online interactions?

_____
_____
_____

Where might you connect with someone in real life for in person connection?

_____
_____
_____

6.8 Managing and working with opposites

In *Wholehearted*, I invite you to explore the idea of working with the duality and tension of opposites. This section provides an opportunity to notice the opposites in your life and interactions, in your writing and creative work and to see what emerges. Here we'll use the power of tarot to begin to tease and map out some of the opposite forces that might be at work in your life and personality.

I mention a few different cards from tarot—The Moon, The Chariot and Temperance. I invite you to spend time reflecting on the images and tapping into your intuition via these cards.

If you have tarot decks available to you, get at least one card representing The Moon, The Chariot and/or Temperance in front of you. If you have a few decks, it is great to look at a few different versions of each card so you can see different images and angles of each archetype. If you don't have physical tarot decks available to you, just google the names of the cards and you will find digital images you can work with.

WHOLEHEARTED LIVING REFLECTIONS

Work first with The Moon. Look at the card and note down what you notice and what comes up for you as you spend time with this card.

_____
_____

Key themes for The Moon are intuition, flow, transitions, imagination, illumination, shifting consciousness, working with unseen forces, synchronicity, cycles.

Ask yourself: Where might the power of intuition, going with the flow and being open to these energies help me with transition and balancing the energy of thinking and being in my head?

Work now with The Chariot. Look at the card and jot down what you notice and what comes up for you.

Key themes for The Chariot are working with opposites, light and dark, forward motion through dealing with or in spite of opposing forces especially the conscious and unconscious, willpower, focus on what needs to be done.

Ask yourself: Where are opposing forces operating in my life? How can I learn from and use the power of these opposing forces to keep me moving forward in my transition journey?

Work next with Temperance. Look at the card and note down what comes up for you as you spend time with this card.

Key themes for Temperance are bringing together tensions and extremes, getting the right or a different mix, bringing opposites together for a different outcome, alchemy, middle ground, creative solutions, your unique blend.

Ask yourself: Where are am I feeling extremes of energy in my life? How can I blend these extremes together or add a dash of something else to create a middle path? How can I hold the tension of opposites to see another way? What areas make up the unique blend of me?

_____

_____

_____

I hope this gives some insights to work with in your life and transition journey. Using opposites to find new options, paths and solutions can be a breakthrough moment that propels you forward.

We will explore working with opposites and the shadow side more fully in Chapter 8.

6.9 Working with natural rhythms and cycles

In *Wholehearted*, I take you through three key ideas for learning to work with natural rhythms and cycles as part of wholehearted self-leadership:

1. Understand your natural preferences for when you work best and harness that.
2. Step up into a wider framework of working with practices and principles.
3. Recognise there are different seasons of life that we need to honour.

Here are some further examples and suggestions for each as guides in your transition journey.

1. Understand your natural preferences for when you work best and harness that.

Here is a little more on my own journey and learning about my own natural preferred rhythms.

Originally, I was trying to squeeze my writing into the work day and the morning would be the most natural way for this to happen. But I already got up at 5:30 am to get out the door at 6:45 am for a long commute, so getting up any earlier was just too much. So I tried to weave writing into the day or at the end when I was tired. I made some progress but not much. It was only when I really committed to changing my life and sought a job-share arrangement to clear up two days a week to write and make a transition that I started to connect with my rhythms.

For the heart of my transition time when I had commitments on a daily basis, I found morning was the best time to write. I got up at about 6 am and worked on my Morning Pages and Tarot Narrative first thing and did my NaNoWriMo work on the *Wholehearted* book initial draft in that time.

Life became a bit freer over time and I didn't get up so early each day, finding rest also important. But I still wrote before doing anything else, to clear the space and settle any tension in my mind helping me to get into sync with what was wanting to come through. Typically, I often get a sense of this in writing my Morning Pages and it will come out more explicitly in the guidance from tarot and oracle work. I weave that story together and I find it often also emerges as a theme in my writing and coaching for the day.

In the final stages of writing *Wholehearted* and this workbook, I have gone back to getting up early to write in the mornings. Co-writing with my friend Beth via Zoom at 5:30 am in bursts of 25 minutes with a chat about writing in between works perfectly. This natural rhythm of waking up early and accountability with another works well for me and helps put what is most important front and centre in each week day.

You can see from my example a mix of trial and error, learning what works for me, working with the circumstances and season I am in, the value of putting what is important in the part of the day that fits my personal rhythms and preferences. Mine happens to be the morning but yours might be the afternoon or evening.

WHOLEHEARTED LIVING REFLECTIONS

What can you draw from my experiences to help you? How might you make changes to the natural rhythm of your day to centre what is important?

You might find Daniel Pink's book *When*[70] a useful resource too. It's all about the scientific secrets to good timing to help us flourish.

2. Step up into a wider framework of working with practices and principles.

Here is a practical example from my morning routines of how I step into a wider framework and connect practices and principles especially working with lunar cycles.

This morning I checked in with the lunar cycle and we have just shifted into the Third Quarter Moon—Yang and the message 'Now that I am receiving, I give back from a place of abundance'. I checked in with Ezzie Spencer's *Lunar Abundance* book so I was fully cognisant of the energies of this cycle and wrote in my Morning Pages about what this means and how I can give back.

Then in my tarot work it was all King of Wands and Ace of Cups and how I can work with mastery over creativity and bring it to fruition in a measured and practical way. The Ace of Cups reminds me it is all about flowing with feeling and self-confidence: the words here, the drafting and the evolving myself as I write. I was reminded to speak my emotional truth with integrity and courage and to let the words flow. Also that there are choices to be made and not to be passive and let things come. It is a Yang phase and I need to be proactive in my choices, be in action and remember to be grateful and give back from that place of flow.

Just as I finished that and went to start writing, an email landed reminding me of the final group call on Ezzie's Book Whispering online project to help bring our books into being. I was able to thank Ezzie directly for her insights that enabled me to begin to get these words down. The natural rhythms and cycles of the morning came full circle so I could express my gratitude directly to a key influence who helped me express my creative self-leadership in this way.

Observe how the practices link up to help me access my inner wisdom and manage my energy in a natural way.

WHOLEHEARTED LIVING REFLECTIONS

Reflect on when you have had a similar experience or how you might weave different energies and cycles into your life.

_____
_____
_____
_____

3. Recognise there are different seasons of life that we need to honour.

There are many ways you can look at the seasons of life, for example:

- struggle, hustle and rest, as outlined in *Wholehearted* from the work of creative coach Jen Carrington[71]
- lunar cycles, menstrual cycles, working within the energies of each month
- the natural seasons of spring, summer, autumn and winter
- the Wheel of the Year and its seasonal festivals such as Samhain and Beltane
- our ageing process and the four seasons of life as women: maiden, mother, maga, crone.

Having these broader frameworks can help us live self-compassionately and wisely.

WHOLEHEARTED LIVING REFLECTIONS

Review this time of your life now with regard to one or more of these natural seasons and rhythms and see how this wisdom can help you with your transition and self-leadership.

Read Julie Parker's book *Priestess* for insights on ancient sacred wisdom for women including the Wheel of the Year and the stages and seasons of women's lives.[72]

6.10 Tuning into intuition and listening within

And you can keep flexing your intuition (because it's like a muscle) to feel into the next right step.

Danielle LaPorte, *White Hot Truth*

Intuition can be a hard thing to pin down and understand, especially if you have a natural preference for what is tangible and knowable through the five senses. Here are some further examples of how intuition works and some practical tips on how you can use intuition to guide creativity and transition. Plus there are some tarot and oracle tips if you want to commence or deepen your intuitive practice.

WHAT INTUITION, ESPECIALLY INTROVERTED, LOOKS LIKE

Dario Nardi's *Neuroscience of Personality*[73] has these tips for working with people with Introverted Intuiting as a cognitive preference to honour this:

- time away from external stimulation and mundane demands ... to access rich internal processes
- a physical or sensory focus
- [help to] verbally or visually communicate the hazy multitude of factors they consider as they arrive at a holistic solution to a problem
- provide techniques for them to turn to when their introspective intuiting process isn't working and they need to act fast
- carve out time to explore the future and visions of what will be. Also work with them to develop specifics to actualize these visions
- encourage rich experiences that feed different brain regions, so when they search within themselves, their brain has something to offer them.

If I translate my tarot and oracle work through this lens, seeing them as tools to access and support Introverted Intuiting, I come up with the following:

- Tarot and oracle reading requires carving out a quiet time and space, usually early in the day. I light a candle, I say a blessing. It is quiet and I am alone. I do the reading, draw on references and pull the story together.
- The cards themselves are beautifully physical and sensory, full of imagery and lovely to hold in a tactile sense. The candle provides light and fragrance.
- I work to record my thoughts and any reading from guidebooks and oracle books including my own Little White Book (LWB) guidebook developed over time from my own wisdom. I gather my thoughts and structure them into a narrative from the symbols that appear or align.
- To help me with my Introverted Intuiting, my reference books, guidebooks and LWB help hone my thoughts as I weave my Introverted Intuiting together. I can do this quite quickly if needed, from the knowledge and experience built up over time.
- Tarot and oracle help me explore visionary insight into what will be and help me actualise these visions in symbols. I might anchor them in a link to a book or crystal to help flesh the potential

thoughts and options into words and images. I write guidance for myself but also for others.
- All of this work feeds different brain regions: reading, visualising, introspection, words, listening within, making meaning, visual thinking, being open to novelty and attention to process, being efficient in doing it each day as a practice, sharing it via social media with words and images and thinking of its presentation in a more extraverted and external way.

This has been my evolving practice and you can see how it has meant I am working from my Introverted Intuiting, connecting the pieces and using it as a form of guidance. Without it, I would have been lost in this time of transition. My intuition has been a source of wisdom and spiritual connection opening up new ways of learning and insight.

WHOLEHEARTED LIVING REFLECTIONS

How might you harness and develop Introverted Intuiting as a support for transition using this example?

_____
_____
_____
_____
_____

What can you take from these tarot and oracle insights to commence or deepen your intuitive practice?

_____
_____
_____
_____
_____

Intuition can also be extraverted, which is more a brainstorming type of process, looking at diverse possible options, scanning widely, looking at connections. How might Extraverted Intuiting be part of your world and practice?

Read 'Introverted and extraverted intuition—how to make intuition a strong practice' on Quiet Writing for further insights.[74]

INTUITION AS A GUIDE: EIGHT WAYS TO WORK IT

Intuition can be a quiet guide in so many ways if we listen to its magic. Here are eight ways to work with intuition that I have discovered are working for me and some questions to prompt you towards how to put it into practice. Granted there might be some thinking and sensing work in there too. It is not a brick wall, but a mode and preference we can shift in and out of, so let your intuition do the talking for a while and see what happens.

WHOLEHEARTED LIVING REFLECTIONS

1. What to read next

What do you need to read now—is it fiction, non-fiction or a combination of both? What does your heart need—to rest with a book, to learn or to be inspired? What do you need to know? What do you want to feel? Are you limiting yourself to just one book when you could be more spontaneous and read more randomly, picking up pieces of wisdom that way?

---

2. What to listen to and when

Do you need music right now or to hear the spoken work like a podcast? What are you tuning into? What do you need to be learning? What random playlist, podcast or subject is calling you or popping up consistently for your attention?

3. Which project to work on next

Of all the projects waving at you for your attention, which one can you work on now with ease and which will be harder? Which one feels right? Even though one might be harder, does that need to be done first even if you are not sure why?

4. When to move and how

Which form of physical exercise will get you moving in the right way to free you up? What environment will ignite your feelings and inspire you? Is it walking to the local cafe, being by the beach, wandering through the bush or walking around the city? Is it yoga, walking, running or cycling? What type of exercise might free up your writing—free-writing, making a list or colouring in first?

5. How to structure your week to best reach your goals

How can you manage your week best to manage self-care and reach your goals? How can it be both enjoyable and productive? Is there anything you can do to find the creative space you need? Which days are best for which projects? How can you reach your goals in ways that work for you?

6. What rhythms in your life will support flow

When do you work best and how can you take advantage of that? How can exercise and movement help establish a rhythm you can take into other areas of your life? What time of day do you work best and how can you make the most of that? What about working with the moon and other cycles to facilitate a balance between receptivity and action?

7. What intuitive tools might help guide you

Which tarot or oracle decks or cards are speaking to you? What about lunar cycles, astrology, spirit guides or quotations that inspire you? How are you working with them and how can you harness their power more effectively?

8. Which combination of influences help you shine your light to help others

Take the time to dream, journal, mind-map, brainstorm, draw, draft, blog or write a poem, to bring together connections for new insights and share them with others to inspire them. Jot down your magical combination of influences and practices here.

Take these learnings and reflections and weave a new narrative through an intuitive and creative way of working and living.

For more on intuition, read *The Inner Tree* by Maura McCarley Torkildson.[75]

6.11 Using the power of language

Language is a fabulous tool for positive self-leadership and wholehearted living. Work through these practical examples and strategies to enhance your awareness of how we use language to downplay ourselves with self-talk and in our interactions. Learn tips for how to rewrite the self-talk to shift the power.

WHOLEHEARTED LIVING REFLECTIONS

WATCHING YOUR USE OF 'PLAYING SMALL' WORDS

Be alert to your use of words such as 'just', 'does that make sense?', 'actually', 'sorry—so sorry'. Observe the impact of them in your correspondence and speech and make an effort to edit them out and see how this feels. Note your feelings and observations here.

_____

_____

_____

WATCHING YOUR USE OF PRESSURE WORDS

Be alert also to words like 'should', 'ought' and 'must', which put pressure on ourselves. Identify where you can choose more self-compassionate words to encourage rather than force yourself.

For example, 'I should get up early in the morning and write' might become 'I could get up early in the morning and write if it aligns with my purpose and energy. It will be different for me but I will give it a go.'

Try rewriting these sentences in more self-compassionate ways and feel the different emotional impact.

I must practise better self-care.

I ought to exercise every day.

I should go to bed earlier.

I must finish writing this book by the end of the year.

FINDING LANGUAGE TO GUIDE US

In *Wholehearted* I also share a list of ways we can use language in a positive way to guide us as a tool for change and to create a lexicon for how we want to manifest ourselves.

WHOLEHEARTED LIVING REFLECTIONS

Revisit this list of examples and identify the ones you can put into action.

- Create a Style Statement (see Chapter 4).
- Be clear on your Core Desired Feelings (see Chapter 4).
- Create a word of the year (or part of the year).
- Define your archetypal blend (see the work of Cerries Mooney).[76]
- Create a personal brand and tagline.
- Use the power of mantras.
- Shape positive affirmations.
- Clearly think about, vocalise or write your intentions.

Which ones call to you as areas to work on now to tap into the power of language as a guide in your transition and life?

———

6.12 Reading for creative influence and personal growth

For this section, I encourage you to do two things to go deeper with looking at reading as a source of creative influence and personal growth:

- read *Reading as Creative Influence*[77] where I take you on a journey of revisiting and honouring the books that influenced me over time.
- scan your life and bookshelves to review what has impacted you in your life and create the chronology of your creative influence and honour your influences.

The steps I took in creating *Reading as Creative Influence* are as follows:

1. Selected key books that have been critical creative and personal influences over the years.
2. Sequenced them in chronological order in the timeline of my life.
3. Spent time with each book to work out the role each book had played in my life and personal narrative.
4. Wrote a short piece on each to create my own book honouring the creative influence.
5. Wrote a reflective essay upfront highlighting key themes and pointing the way to the development of my own voice and the work I want to create.

It's deep work. I set out to write a piece from this work and ended up with a ninety-four-page book. But do the work in whatever way works for you. The main thing is to honour creative influence in your life and how this special blend of you and others can take you forward as a guide in transition times.

WHOLEHEARTED LIVING REFLECTIONS

To get you started:

Jot down the titles of the books that have had a lasting impact on you over time or that were critical at key turning point moments.

Begin to put them in chronological order in terms of your life.

Choose one and free-write about its influence on you.

We will explore creative influence more in 7.1.

6.13 Prioritising movement, exercise and self-care

In *Wholehearted* I share how movement and exercise have been a central support in my transition journey. It can be a much underrated area we connect narrowly with being fit or losing weight, but it is far more than just the physical benefits. The mental health impacts can be immense.

Take some time here to reflect on your relationship with movement, exercise and self-care. It might be positive; it might need some work. But spend time with it and see where it might take you.

WHOLEHEARTED LIVING REFLECTIONS

What movement and forms of exercise feature in your life now?

_____
_____
_____

What is your relationship with movement and exercise as a form of self-care?

_____
_____
_____

What forms of movement and exercise did you love as a child?

_____
_____
_____

Where could you weave movement and exercise more into your life in ways that you love?

_____

_____

What might be the benefits of this?

_____

_____

Where will you go? What will you do? Who will you do it with?

_____

_____

When will you start?

_____

_____

6.14 Being unattached to outcomes

This is a tricky area to understand. It is a subtle understanding of the difference between power and force. The key themes are conscious allowing, yin, letting things come to you, being shaped, reflecting, resisting expectations and co-creating with spirit and others. We often hear about 'getting out of our own way', which implies we don't always know the best way for ourselves and this can be hard to accept.

The secret is understanding the power of not being attached to outcomes is knowing how it interacts with intentions. Working with our higher self and guides that know more than we do is part of this too.

Working with coaching clients, I see how this plays out. A client comes with a goal of wanting to write a novel or create a blog. That may be what they want at that time but as they go through coaching, they realise what they really want is to carve out creative space and freedom when in a situation of prioritising work or others' needs ahead of their own.

You see it time and time again in coaching. A woman sets her goals and then other things emerge. But without the initial goal-setting and taking time for coaching, the deeper needs and outcomes would not have emerged. So the initial desired outcome is one thing and what emerges is another. Often both are achieved.

The key is to set your desired feelings and intentions and then commit to showing up to that and see what emerges. It is not always what you expect. It is often more than you know at the time. The act of setting the intention or goal sets the process in motion and then what happens is a response to that. We need to learn to be open to the signs and symbols that emerge as we go down the path of bringing that intention to life. Sometimes we need to reorient and work with a coach or with intuitive tools that can help us see what we cannot see ourselves on this path.

This applies to the outcomes of our work in the world and how we can be of service to others too. Often we desire specific success-based outcomes like a certain income and *x* number of clients. But if we operate from this mindset, our energy shifts and we might not come from an energy of attraction and abundance. Tapping into our deeper desires and meaning about what we wish to shape can create success beyond measure.

WHOLEHEARTED LIVING REFLECTIONS

What does being unattached to outcomes mean to you?

Can you think of times when you have set an intention or desired feeling and the outcome has been different from what you expected?

What did you learn from this?

How can you open yourself to being more unattached to outcomes, reducing your specific expectations about what might happen?

How might you practically allow the universe to express its power and wisdom in your life rather than you forcing it?

Finally, look at areas where you are in service to others and the outcomes you are specifying as measures of success, such as income or numbers of clients.

How can you connect in deeper ways with abundance for both yourself and your clients?

What is your deeper mission in life and how can that drive you?

What might be the deeper measures of success that can support you?

6.15 Honouring practice, ritual and experimentation

It is a combination of structure and routine, showing up and mixing this with experimentation and creativity. But the container of regularity and practice is a solid cradle for inspiration.

Wholehearted: Self-leadership for Women in Transition

Practice, ritual and experimentation are important elements in a wholehearted life. You decide on or try out elements like writing, movement and intuitive work and then play with them to find the unique combination that works for you. And it is in the interplay between showing up—routine, practice, regularity, ritual—and how you show up, with a spirit of curiosity, experimentation, sacred engagement where the richness and growth lie.

EXPERIMENTING WITH MORNING PAGES

I've shared different aspects of my Morning Pages practice in *Wholehearted* and this workbook and here I want to focus on the experimentation that the practice of Morning Pages provides.

Reflecting via Morning Pages about whether writing is a practice that enables me or keeps me from other activities and projects, I wrote a list of what Morning Pages helps me to do:

- settle my rattling thoughts and externalise them, putting them on paper so I can see them
- work out what is worrying me and challenging me
- celebrate my wins
- set goals and see what is important
- identify emerging creative thoughts and focus
- capture ideas and make plans for the day, week, month, year
- work with the cycles of the moon and be in flow.

You can see that it is a practice that embodies experimentation and discovery. They are powerful outcomes for a practice that takes about twenty to thirty minutes. You have to counter that 'I just want to get on with things' feeling, which is strong and will keep coming at you. But you can see from this list that it is a place for experimenting and seeing what happens in a spirit of curiosity. The more you show up over time, the greater the opportunity to go deeper with your practice.

EXPERIMENTING WITH TAROT

Also via Morning Pages I thought about the value of tarot and brainstormed a list of what Tarot Narrative actually does as a practice. It started with the words, 'Oh, what this does not do as a practice', so its importance was immediately recognisable and apparent.

My Tarot Narrative practice helps me to:

- learn about myself
- tap into guidance that is around and within
- connect with my intuition in a focused and grounded way
- craft a self-leadership narrative for my life
- notice what is beneath the surface of my awareness
- learn more about tarot and intuition
- learn to channel and connect with spiritual guides and supporters
- connect with archetypal knowledge and symbols
- practice extending my introverted intuiting practice to others
- connect with others on spiritual and creative planes and projects
- discover and connect in with parts of myself and be more wholehearted
- keep in tune with my own rhythms and cycles—yin and yang, cycles of the moon
- set intentions and be aware of the best areas and ways to set intentions
- learn to write intuitively
- be the queen of my thoughts and quiet my mind.

These ways of working with tarot did not emerge overnight. They developed from an ongoing engagement. You can see how commitment to practice creates an incubator for experimenting and going further and deeper on many levels.

WHOLEHEARTED LIVING REFLECTIONS

Choose an example in your life where you have shown up in a practice over time. It could be running, horse-riding, writing, art, tarot, rock-climbing, astrology, coaching, teaching or any other practice that you keep working at. Make a list, like my lists, of the value of that practice and what it has helped you to do.

_____
_____
_____
_____
_____

Choose an area where you can deliberately experiment more through your practice over time. How might you play and approach it with curiosity and a spirit of experimentation?

_____
_____
_____
_____

7

VALUING AND BUILDING INFLUENCES AND CONNECTIONS

7.1 Influences and creative connections: what brought you to here

> *How we choose to pay attention, and relate to information and each other shapes who we become, shapes our creative destiny and, in turn, shapes our experience of the world.*
>
> **Maria Popova, *Networked Knowledge and Combinatorial Creativity*[78]**

Here are some thoughts and tips on honouring our special creative influences, connecting them with our passions and taking them forward into new endeavours. I also invite you to begin to identify, explore and honour your unique influences through a series of reflection prompts and tips.

THE CREATIVE INFLUENCE OF WHAT WE LOVE

Knowing and honouring our creative influences is how we connect with our legacy and passions and take them forward. How creative influences shape us, our world and our own creations is a key theme in *Reading as Creative Influence*,[79] as discussed in 6.12 via a personal journey of reviewing the books that have impacted me over my life.

I've always been acutely aware of creative influence and how each book I read makes some kind of impact on me. Perhaps it's my INTJ personality and that mix of Introverted Intuiting and Extraverted Thinking, or maybe it's my language and literature background. From a young age, I've always read deeply, kept notes and chronicled influences—whether it be music, the written word, images or art. Many of us seek ways to capture what influences us, what speaks to us, what leaves a lasting impression in ways that make sense for us.

Here are some of mine and the questions and feelings that emerge from these deep connections:

- Why does Daphne du Maurier—her books, where she lived, everything about her—capture my heart so much?
- When I hear The Cure's 'A Forest', why do I get all shivery each time, even though I've listened to it many times? Why do I cry every time I hear 'What a Wonderful World'? And why does the song 'Wichita Lineman' do things to the top of my head that I can't explain?
- And visually, why do artist Edward Hopper's austere landscapes and solitary figures connect with me so intensely? Why do I feel like I exactly understand 'The Scream' by Edvard Munch? And why does the light in Ansel Adam's photographs bring me to tears?

You could say I'm just sensitive. But all of us have had that feeling of reading, listening, seeing and engaging with all of our senses, witnessing something deep, visceral and connected with an artist, writer or place. Those influences stay with us and they gather, coalesce and merge into something unique within us, connecting with other aspects of our personality and passions.

COMBINATORIAL CREATIVITY

In *Networked Knowledge and Combinatorial Creativity*, Maria Popova explores the notion of creativity as a combination of influences. Popova introduces us to the idea of a *florilegium* from the 14th century. These florilegia were:

> compilations of excerpts from other writings, essentially mashing up selected passages and connecting dots from existing texts to illuminate a specific topic or doctrine or idea. The word comes from the Latin for "flower" and "gather."[80]

She provides examples of where knowledge or skill in one sphere influenced and sharpened another. For example, novelist Vladimir Nabokov collected butterflies, an activity which he believed helped with creating detail and precision in his writing.

Here are a few concepts tied up in the idea of combinatorial creativity:

1. different areas of knowledge and influence can come together to impact on each other in new ways.
2. nothing is completely new from the ground up, but more a consequence of influences coming together and how we integrate or collate them in our unique way.
3. all that connected knowledge and skill creates a body of mastery we can call on to connect the dots further into new creations.

As I explore in *Reading as Creative Influence,* the books we choose to read at any time, their influence on us, the ones that make a huge personal impact and the interaction of this with our context and story, all play critical roles. It is fascinating to step back and reflect on the books that really moved you and why; the ones you keep close by and why they are always there.

In her essay 'Honor Your Lineage' in *Fierce on the Page*,[81] Sage Cohen talks about books as teachers. Just as special teachers and mentors in our lives impact on us and leave a legacy we take forward, so books are special teachers whose messages we need to honour.

HOW DO YOU HONOUR YOUR INFLUENCES?

So how do you honour your influences? I am a big believer in acknowledging influences and the impact of others. I think it is important to take the time to acknowledge who has influenced and helped you. I also believe strongly in acknowledging others' work you are referring to, drawing from or weaving into your own. Perhaps it's my academic background with all those essays and bibliographies and references annotated, though in the workplace, too, I would always acknowledge the contribution and influence of others. I'd talk about the outcomes of projects as the collation of the team's influence as much as any leadership on my part, such is my antenna about valuing influence.

So let's begin to explore your creative influences.

WHOLEHEARTED LIVING REFLECTIONS

Think of the musicians or writers, books or songs that you love. Why of all the musicians and writers do some speak to you so directly and passionately?

_____

_____

Whose books are close by you in your literary lineage altar speaking to you now and for many years?

_____

_____

Which songs make the hair on the back of your neck stand on end?

_____

_____

Which songs or books are linked to significant events in your life?

What role did they play and why was it important?

What poems speak to your heart and why?

Why do you listen to every podcast of a certain creative influencer?

And whose courses, podcasts or books have you gone back to as the key creative and entrepreneurial influences in your life?

Scanning our creative influences helps us see key themes over time. It can also help us see what is missing and what we need to do next. I became aware of how most of the books in my list of creative influences are by white authors. I need to be diversifying my reading to embrace more Black Indigenous Women of Colour authors especially. In this way, I am ensuring I am being creatively influenced and inclusive in my reading choices over time and this informs my reading priorities now and into the future.

WHOLEHEARTED LIVING REFLECTIONS

What comes to attention as a gap in your creative influence now? How can you begin to bridge it?

CREATIVE, PERSONAL AND ENTREPRENEURIAL INFLUENCE

Here are a few further practical tips for knowing, honouring and acknowledging your influences:

1 Take the time to identify your influences

- Collect influences from different genres in your life (music, books, movies) and see how they connect to identify the common themes in your life.
- Identify the people (famous figures, online connections, teachers, family, friends) who have had the most influence on you. Think about their impact and why it was important.

2 Thank your influencers

- Publicly or privately (or both), take the time to acknowledge and thank the people who have influenced you for their contribution to your journey.
- We don't always know when we are having an influence. Taking the time to tell others of their impact can be something that buoys their creativity for their next effort. It gives strength to their work and channels more energy for their contribution.

- Sometimes we might not be able to thank people directly. But show gratitude for their work in some way such as acknowledging sources in a written piece. This allows others to learn from them and integrate it into their own creative journey.

3   Acknowledge influence and the source of ideas in your own work

- If you quote someone else's words or reference someone else's thoughts, make sure it is properly and correctly attributed. Don't claim others work as your own. Honour the creator by quoting and attributing their words correctly.
- Don't be afraid to mention who has influenced you because it's all part of that rich combination of ideas and dots that brings new connections to life.

4   Wear your influences with pride and originality

- Boy George, when a judge on *The Voice* television program in Australia, said to one of the contestants: 'You need to wear your influences—they make you who you are.' As you connect the dots of your influences in new ways, wear them in ways only you can, to create your unique work in the world.
- Just as we can dress creatively, putting together different styles like modern and vintage, wear your unique influences confidently and proudly. Make your own style statement.
- Look for connections, common themes and even the tension of opposites as sources of creativity. In this way, you can create your personal signature in how you work and present yourself.

5   Work through jealousy and envy

- A huge killer of combinatorial creativity is feeling jealous about the work of others that draws from similar influences. You have a great idea and then you see someone doing a very similar thing. You can feel gutted and overcome with envy.
- Work through this so your unique perspective is not lost. You might have very similar sets of passions and influences to someone

else. But the way they are blended with your unique personality and experiences will always be individual. So find your own way and have confidence in your unique remix and personal style.
- You could connect with the person and celebrate their strengths. You could share their work, see how you can work together and find new ways to co-create from these shared influences. Acknowledge the envy and work from a sense of abundance, not limited thinking. More on working through envy in 8.5.

HAVE THE COURAGE TO DO YOUR OWN WORK

At the end of the day, we need to have the courage to do our own work. The best way we can take all those antecedents and influences forward is to honour them in new creations. Finding ways to identify our special perspective, our niche, our unique way of working is a creative act all of its own.

As Steven Pressfield reminds us in *The War of Art*:

> Creative work is not a selfish act or a bid for attention on the part of the actor. It's a gift to the world and every being in it. Don't cheat us of your contribution. Give us what you've got.[82]

WHOLEHEARTED LIVING REFLECTIONS

Which of the above practical tips for knowing, honouring and acknowledging your influences resonate with you? How will you put them into practice?

7.2 Online creative influences and mentors

You've read through my top five online creative influences and mentors on my journey in *Wholehearted*. Creative influences and mentors come in many forms. You might find online influences have been key as I have focused on here; it might be in-person influences or a mix of both. Reflect on who has influenced you and how and take some time to tease out their impact and role in your wholehearted ways of being.

WHOLEHEARTED LIVING REFLECTIONS:

Who has influenced you? Who are the online or in-person creative influencers and mentors that have helped you on your path?

What has each taught you or inspired in you?

What other role models, ancestors, family members, famous people, historical figures, authors, artists or bloggers have influenced you?

What is their legacy? What have they taught you?

_____
_____
_____
_____

Using the tips in 7.1 of this workbook, make a list of strategies for how you might practically honour and acknowledge your influences as part of your creative and transition journey.

_____
_____
_____
_____

7.3 Finding our community

From reading Chapter 7 of *Wholehearted*, you can see how finding our community can be a rich mix at times of transition as we seek deeper and new ways of connecting. Take a step back and think about your community, where you are now and what else you might like to build in as a form of support and also giving back.

WHOLEHEARTED LIVING REFLECTIONS

Who are you connected to now and how do they support you?

_____
_____
_____
_____

Where are there gaps in your knowledge or connections and how can you fill that?

What is your relationship to social media and online resources and influences?

How do you see online avenues as a source of connection to inspire your creativity and transition? How might you grow this?

How can you develop in-person connections and networks in a deeper way?

8

WORKING WITH THE SHADOW SIDE IN BECOMING WHOLE

8.1 Exploring the shadow side

In *Wholehearted*, I share some ideas on thinking about the shadow side of our lives—our weaknesses and less preferred areas and ways of operating. I also highlight that even our strengths, when overdone, can become weaknesses or blind spots. Think of the person who is very organised and prefers tidiness to disorder who is typically very calm but flies off the handle when anyone else moves anything or doesn't put things back in the right place. We all have the potential for spaces like this in our lives and self-awareness of them is a fabulous place to start.

So take some time to reflect on these questions. Brainstorm, journal, mind-map, free-write or list—whatever works for you as you traverse into terrain that is not always super comfortable!

WHOLEHEARTED LIVING REFLECTIONS

Where might a 'shadow career' be operating or have operated in your life? Why?

_____

_____

What do you know you need to develop? For example, skills, knowledge, experience, emotions.

Which complementary areas do you need to foster to create balance in your life?

What is out of balance? What is a no-go zone where you feel uncomfortable?

What are your weaker areas? What comes up straight away as a weak area, sore point, skill lacking?

How would you answer the 'What is your greatest weakness?' question? Think interview situation.

What is your Achilles heel? What do you hate? What buttons can others push easily, knowingly or unknowingly?

Where might your strengths, when overdone, become a weakness or blind spot?

What strengths do you have that might feel like a weakness at times?

How can working on your weaknesses together with your strengths make you more well-rounded?

Try out the online Saboteur Questionnaire for insight into how you self-sabotage.[83] It's available at https://www.positiveintelligence.com/assessments/. This also includes insights on how our strengths can become a source of self-sabotage.

Go gently with this, as it is zeroing in on some negative behaviours, but view it in a positive way: you are gaining self-awareness into behaviour that might otherwise be happening without you knowing. Getting a higher and clearer perspective on these behaviours helps you make better and wiser self-leadership choices. Jot some notes down about what you learn.

8.2 Wholeness, balance and shadow times in our life

In *Wholehearted*, I encourage you to think back upon the times in your life when the most growth occurred. Not all growth stems from difficult times, but it is often the case that we learn and reach for creative expression at extreme times, like when we experience loss or disappointment or become ill.

WHOLEHEARTED LIVING REFLECTIONS

Think of the timelines in your life. When was the biggest growth or most creative time? What did you learn from this time?

_____
_____
_____
_____
_____

I also share examples of women's stories from the *Wholehearted Stories* series on Quiet Writing. Here are some you may wish to read to reflect on the experience of transformation and creativity through challenge:

> Lynn Hanford-Day's story *Breakdown to Breakthrough*[84]
> Kerstin Pilz's story *Grief and Pain Can Be Our Most Important Teachers*[85]
> Jade Herriman's story *Embracing a Creative Life*[86]
> Sally Morgan's story *Writing the Way Through*[87]

Make some notes on what you learn from their stories and how they might connect with your own story.

_____
_____

What insights from the shadow times in your life come forward for your deeper attention?

_____
_____
_____
_____

8.3 Shadows of type: unconscious and inferior functions

Progress towards integration and discovery of the self can often be seen in people during the period that Jung called midlife, when they become more open to the other aspects of their personalities, ideas and experiences that would have previously been in conflict with their egos and self-images.

Angelina Bennet, The Shadows of Type[88]

In section 8.3 of *Wholehearted*, I introduce you to some psychological type frameworks of what is less conscious and self-aware in our personalities. Here are some more detailed explorations with practical examples. They show how psychological type is a powerful framework for understanding and beginning to integrate the less preferred and more unconscious aspects of personality. This is often the work of midlife. I focus on my INTJ psychological type preferences here as an example.

I mention in *Wholehearted* the four main cognitive functions and the other four complementary functions which are the mirror and the opposite or shadow of the four main ones. Remember too the recent research by Moody, Majors and Barimany[89] that has highlighted that all eight aspects of our personality are playing out at any one time.

As a taste of what psychological type insights offer, here is a map of my type—INTJ—and its typical preferences:

Function	Preferences for INTJ
Dominant/superior function	Introverted Intuition
Auxiliary function	Extraverted Thinking
Tertiary function	Introverted Feeling
Inferior function	Extraverted Sensing
Shadow of superior function	Extraverted Intuition
Shadow of auxiliary function	Introverted Thinking
Shadow of tertiary function	Extraverted Feeling
Shadow of inferior function	Introverted Sensing

Each of the psychological types will have a similar indicative map of preferences; but how we actually work with our preferences is another story unique to each of us. Gaining a meta-awareness of our personality can be a powerful tool and construct for self-knowledge and self-awareness. Have a think about these questions and jot down some notes.

WHOLEHEARTED LIVING REFLECTIONS

Why do you think we often repeat the same patterns over and over in our life?

What potential might be trying to get out but is stuck behind unhelpful manifestations like envy, fear or feelings of scarcity?

WHAT INSIGHTS PSYCHOLOGICAL TYPE OFFERS

Personality is dynamic, and psychological type helps us see how these cognitive preferences might be playing out. It can also help us see the hidden potential and opportunities for deeper self-knowledge.

An area where we often have blocks and blind spots is the inferior function. Our lead function in our type, as Dario Nardi reminds us, remains 'the captain of our ship'[90] or driver of our car. Our inferior function is like the infant in the baby seat as Angelina Bennet describes:

> *Although the baby is usually asleep and unnoticed, sometimes it will emit offensive odours and unpleasant substances, and the boot of the car may be full of baby baggage. However, when the baby wakes up and screams, the car's passengers, and in particular the driver, is sent into chaos until the baby's needs are met.*[91]

Naomi Quenk describes this phenomenon of when the 'other' in us emerges and confuses us as being 'in the grip'.[92] We often experience it when we are tired or stressed and it can make us look long and hard at who we are and why we are behaving that way. These moments can be an opportunity to gain new information and insights about ourselves and the hidden potential within. The opposite to our strongest function is a source of balance and self-knowledge if we can work out ways to engage with it despite the discomfort.

AN EXAMPLE: INTJ, INTROVERTED INTUITION AND EXTRAVERTED SENSING

Each personality type has that preferred dominant function that is the captain of our ship and an inferior function that we will typically run a mile from, especially when younger.

As an INTJ, my dominant function is Introverted Intuition and I am very happy in the world of connections, patterns and theories, especially when I work them out myself in the quiet of my own inner world. There is no coincidence that my business is called *Quiet Writing*—it is the place where all the action happens and where my gift to the world is shaped and developed.

My inferior function—the opposite of my dominant—is Extraverted Sensing. This is the world of living for the moment, being oriented to action and fun, appreciating variety, surprise and things changing rapidly. It is also activated in the external world, with people or in the natural world of things and events.

Now you would think this is a fabulous way to be and it is. But it is not my natural way. I hate surprises. I like to know what is coming at me. I am not action-oriented, not without thinking about it a lot anyway. And I am much happier without too much stimulation of a sensory kind, especially too much at once.

But in this more shadowy space of my type is growth, opportunity, wholeness and adaptability. I know my home base and preferences very well as an INTJ and I am very comfortable there. But growth lies both in taking my strengths forward and embracing and integrating my inferior function. My first blog was called *Transcending*, and this whole concept of integrating our less preferred and shadow aspects tends to develop as we head towards middle life. I started my first blog in 2010 when I was 49.

As Mary McGuiness explains in her book *You've Got Personality*, for people with INTJ preferences in midlife, aged thirty-five to fifty-five:

> During Midlife, the Fourth function, extraverted Sensing, will develop. Now INTJs turn their attention to the outer world of reality, facts, details, and sensory experience. They will be more

observant of details and will often engage in activities that stimulate the senses, sights, sounds or smells. Some may engage in physical exercise and outdoor walks, enjoying the sensory experience. They may become more interested in health and keeping the body in shape. They may take up new activities like craft, often designing their own ways of doing things. Sometimes, these activities will stimulate them to write in a journal or diary. INTJs will now be more comfortable living in the present and dealing with reality, but they will still focus on setting and achieving goals and obtaining recognition for their effort. They will still like to live in an orderly way.[93]

All of this is very true for me. I swim in the ocean a few times a week, a practice started a few years ago at the age of fifty-five. This Extraverted Sensing experience has been vital in keeping me balanced and grounded as I have gone through a time of major transition. I have become much more interested in and committed to modifying my diet, yoga, walking, strengthening my body as well as my mind. I'm enjoying dealing with the present more in my business. But I still don't like surprises and orderly is definitely my preferred way of being and working. Our lead function is still the captain of our ship and a clue to our strengths we can use as an actor and guide as we evolve.

WHOLEHEARTED LIVING REFLECTIONS

What thoughts arise for you from reading this case study and from your knowledge of your personality?

_____
_____
_____
_____

If you would like to learn more about the inferior function and how it works, read Sue Blair's article 'Invoking the Inferior Function'[94] and jot down any insights that occur.

If you know your type, make some notes on your inferior function, what you might learn from it and how you might progress this.

I have just touched on the edge of insights from psychological type in this section. Psychological type is a great way to be more conscious about your blind spots and to increase self-awareness on what can help balance and ground you, especially in midlife. If you would like to explore in more detail, I encourage you to reach out to me via Personality Stories Coaching[95] to begin this deeper self-leadership journey.

8.4 Grief, loss and peak experiences

We have touched on the more challenging aspects of life and what they might have taught us in 8.2, but here we look at some specific examples of grief and loss and what they might teach us. I shared my own experiences of two peak times in my life, a story of unrequited love when I was younger and my experience of tragic loss when my brother died. Both taught me so much, though I wish I had learned these lessons in less painful and terribly sad ways.

I asked some questions of unrequited love experiences that you might have also experienced. They are useful to explore even if it was some time ago.

WHOLEHEARTED LIVING REFLECTIONS

Some questions we might ask if we find ourselves experiencing unrequited love at any time in our life are:

What is it we are yearning for and seeking in the shape of another person?

_____

_____

What are we hoping that person will bring us and how can we give it to ourselves in a more sustainable way?

_____

_____

What is there in that anima/animus projection? What aspects of the masculine (or feminine) are we desiring—independence? self-leadership? strength? direction? And how we can manifest it ourselves?

_____

_____

In the wake of loss and rejection, what story is being told? What creative urges are surfacing and how can we honour them?

_____

_____

How are we seeking to be wholehearted through the love and time with another and how can we be wholehearted in ourselves?

_____

_____

Experiences of grief and loss can be painful to go back to and they may be more recent or raw for you. So go very gently with these reflections and honour where you are now. But I encourage you to take some time to honour what these difficult times have taught you as a way of helping you to move more positively through challenging times.

For this reflection, I encourage you to free-write and let this experience speak to you so you can see what emerges.
What has grief and loss taught you and how can you take these experiences forward positively in your life?

8.5 Envy and what wants to come through

In *Wholehearted*, I focus on the lessons of envy and what wants to come through as guides for wholehearted self-leadership, and I share tips for dealing with envy. From working with coaching clients, I know that envy might not be an issue for you or it might be something you have already worked through significantly. But there might be some other negative emotion that works similarly in your life. It might be one of the other six 'deadly sins': pride, greed, lust, gluttony, wrath, sloth—or something else you are acutely aware of.

So use my tips to interrogate envy—or work through another negative emotion of your choice—via the below prompts and questions.

WHOLEHEARTED LIVING REFLECTIONS

1. See envy as a valuable guide to what you really want

Take some time here to interrogate envy, ask it questions, dialogue with it, write about it to see what it is telling you about what you aspire to. You might start with: 'What are you trying to tell me, envy?' and then keep asking it questions.

2. Call it out as envy and just notice it, then put it aside

How can you put envy in its place so that it is not where you work or create from?

3. Find a way to talk about envy

Where might you initiate a conversation about feeling envious of someone where it feels okay to have this conversation? Or how can you initiate a conversation about envy with a more objective third person such as a coach or loved one to help get the feelings out?

4. Tackle envy head on by acting on the feelings in a positive way

Where might it be appropriate to reach out to people and admire their work and see ways you can collaborate or work constructively?

_____
_____
_____

5. Learn from the envy and act on its lessons

If someone is doing what you want to be doing, learn from them and plan your own way with their experiences as your model and support, directly or indirectly.

What might you learn from another whose work resonates with what you desire to create?

_____
_____
_____
_____

6. Remember your unique blend and take on the world

The way you do things will be uniquely shaped by you, as no one else has had the exact same experiences and influences as you. How does this insight make you feel?

_____
_____

7. **Use it or lose it**

Remember, as Elizabeth Gilbert reminds us in *Big Magic*, there is also an element of 'use it or lose it'.[96] Where might realising and remembering this help you overcome blockages and move ahead?

8. **Stay in your own lane**

How might you remind yourself to stay in your own lane and keep focused on your own journey?

9. **Create an envy or jealousy map**

Create an envy or jealousy map to identify what you want to bring forth and create. Identify in line with Julia Cameron's *The Artist's Way* activity[97]: who you are envious of, why and what the Action Antidote is to help you see how you can use the experience positively and learn from it.

8.6 Working with polarities

In *Wholehearted*, I share the advantages of actively working with opposites in our lives including a number of examples of polarities. I invite you now to identify how working with polarities might be helpful in your self-leadership journey of transition.

Here are the key ones I mention, working through the first four in detail:

1. Yin and yang
2. Head and heart
3. Masculine and feminine energy
4. Movement and stillness
5. Dark and light
6. Introvert and extravert
7. Intuitive and sensing
8. Planned and spontaneous

Choose one of these polarities or another that calls to you and explore how working with these opposites might help you gain balance and strength.

8.7 Choosing to shed skins

I highlight in section 8.7 of *Wholehearted* how our transition journeys can be a moving away from what is successful. We might choose to shed skins we are comfortable in such as jobs where we are well-recompensed or other situations where we experience security and have been successful. These definitions of success might no longer fulfil us and we realise it is time to shift. Here we explore the idea of abandoned success in your life to help you move on.

WHOLEHEARTED LIVING REFLECTIONS

Where has the idea of 'abandoned success' played out in your life?

Why is it sometimes hard to step away or plan a path from what is successful or comfortable?

What challenges does this pose?

Reflect on the Eight of Cups tarot card. Get a version or multiple versions of the card in front of you from your own tarot decks or online images and see what the symbolism of this card brings forward for you. Journal on it here and honour this energy in your life—past, present and future.

_____
_____
_____
_____

8.8 The cost of feeling partial and the business of the heart

In *Wholehearted*, I talk about where we go through immense pain and suffering and feel partial. Take some time here to reflect on where you might be choosing to feel partial and can decide to feel more whole by processing and integrating pain and suffering in more positive ways.

WHOLEHEARTED LIVING REFLECTIONS

Identify an area in the present or past where you might have felt less than whole over time because of something that happened. It might be a death of someone close to you, being diagnosed with a chronic illness, mental health issues, heartbreak or not getting something you desperately desired.

Note it down here and reflect on how you felt or feel partial from that event.

_____
_____

How can you see this situation anew?

How can you practise self-compassion as you move through what can be most challenging in our lives?

8.9 Open-hearted change and being a work in progress

Sometimes change is simply hard and acknowledging that helps. Seeing ourselves as a work in progress and recognising that we need to revisit areas of learning or view habits in different ways to finally crack the solution can help. If we take the perspective of life as a spiralling journey where experiences and lessons repeat in new ways but at higher vantage points and different perspectives, that can feel better. The experiences are not lost. We are learning more and more, and keeping an open heart and beginner's mind can keep us positive and growing.

WHOLEHEARTED LIVING REFLECTIONS

What are some examples of where change just feels or has felt plain hard in your life?

What makes it so hard?

Where can you take the perspective of a spiralling story of change over time and see where you have made progress and not be so hard on yourself?

What can you learn from repeated patterns?

Reflect on ways you can embrace the mindset of being a 'work in progress' and having a beginner's mind to break through areas where you are stuck or working from self-limiting beliefs. Explore some of the tarot cards mentioned in 8.9 in *Wholehearted* for some ideas: The Fool, the Seven of Swords or the Eight of Wands.

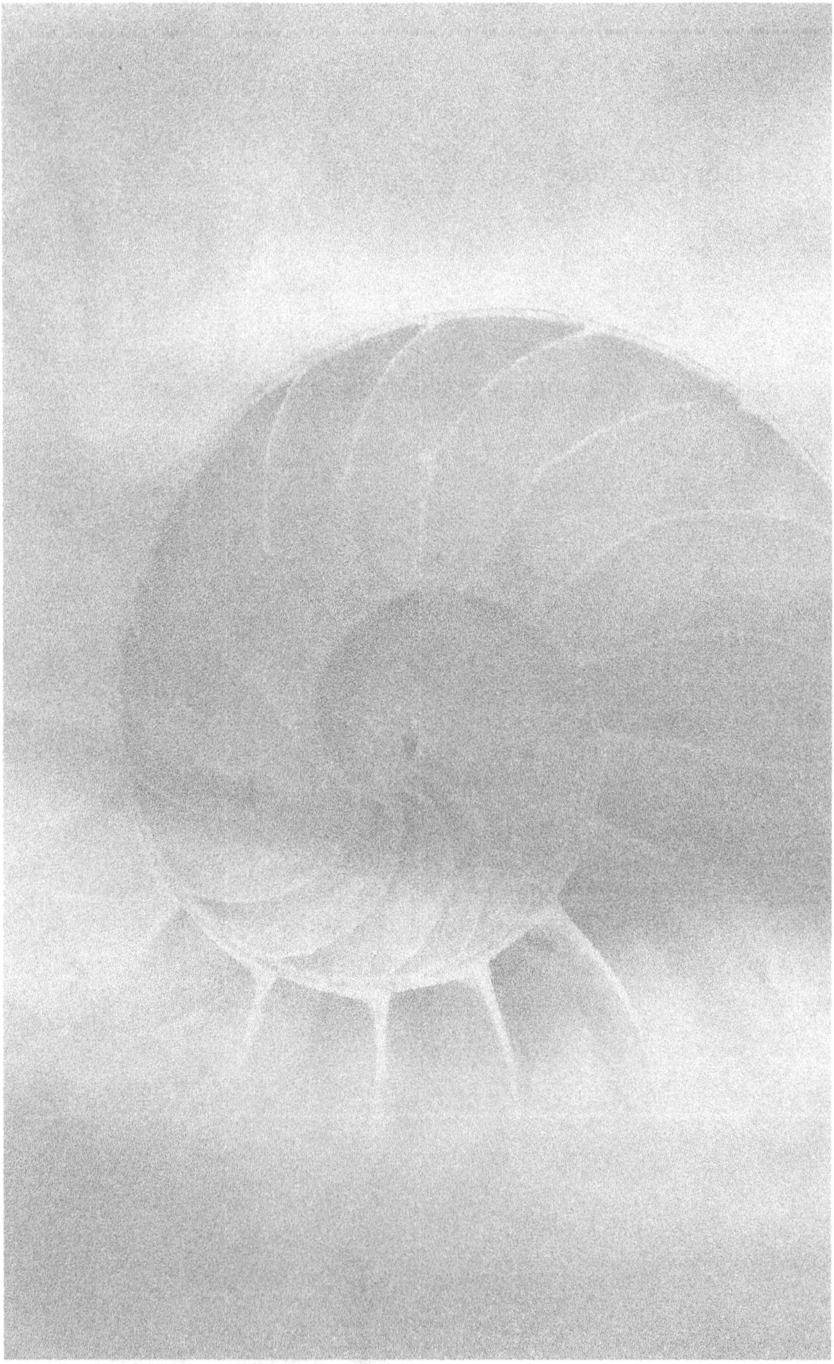

PART THREE

BRINGING IT ALL TOGETHER

9

GUIDES FOR THE WHOLEHEARTED LIVING PATH

9.1 Synchronicity of spirit and the art of human experience

In *Wholehearted*, I identify two important guides on the path of wholehearted living. Synchronicity is the first of these. Here, we look at synchronicity, examples in your life and how you might become more fluent in the language of symbols.

WHOLEHEARTED LIVING REFLECTIONS

Reflect on where you have experienced moments of synchronicity in your life and note down a few key times.

_____
_____
_____
_____

Choose one of these to work through in more detail as I did in 9.1 of *Wholehearted*. It might be a one-off example or it might be a deeper recurring engagement with synchronicity. Sometimes too we have periods of our life when synchronous experiences abound. That can be very worthwhile to reflect on.

What was special about this synchronous experience or series of experiences?

_____
_____
_____
_____

What did you learn from it and what was the message for your life?

_____
_____
_____
_____

One aspect of synchronicity is that it is like a language we can become more fluent in—developing the art of reading symbols and noticing connections.

How have you developed your fluency in this area?

_____
_____
_____
_____

How might you grow this ability to tap into the higher power of synchronicity?

_____
_____
_____

9.2 Grounding in the practical and everyday

The second guide for the wholehearted living path is identifying the acts and practices that bring you home to yourself in the everyday. Working out how you can engage in these activities more consciously to guide your path through the ups and downs of circumstance to a more wholehearted life is time well spent. They will be powerful anchors you can turn to in the swirly uncertainty of change.

WHOLEHEARTED LIVING REFLECTIONS

Reflect on how you might ground yourself into the practical, embedding these practices in your life via these questions.

Think about times of change in your life. How did you find ways to ground yourself in the practical and everyday?

What self-leadership practices and anchors do you have in place now to ground you in each day? Read my list in 9.2 of *Wholehearted* for ideas.

Make two lists: 'What works for me' and 'What doesn't work for me'. Do more of what works for you and less of what doesn't work for you. Keep adding to the lists over time and keep them handy as a resource to keep yourself grounded.

How can you consciously build time for the activities and practices that work for you into your life and schedule?

How can you be more grateful for these everyday grounding experiences and honour them in your life?

10

SELF-LEADERSHIP AND LOVE AS THE HEART OF WHOLEHEARTEDNESS

Chapter 10 of *Wholehearted* focuses on where we have choice and how we can exercise it in our lives. It is easy to focus on where we feel limited. But we can all exercise stronger self-leadership and make more powerful and conscious choices whatever our circumstances. I hope all of the strategies and tips shared in *Wholehearted* and this workbook help you to put this into practice for a more wholehearted life in line with what you love and desire to create.

Reflect on the choices you have and what transition invites in your life to round off the workbook reflections.

WHOLEHEARTED LIVING REFLECTIONS

In what areas of your life do you not have choice?

_____
_____
_____

What is the impact of feeling like you don't have a choice?

_____
_____

Take a step back and reflect on where you do have choice.

Make a list of areas where you can exercise more choice and self-leadership now.

_____
_____
_____
_____
_____

Which stands out to you as the top three areas that can make the biggest difference?

_____
_____
_____
_____

How does the concept of self-leadership make you feel different?

_____
_____
_____
_____
_____

How can you exercise stronger self-leadership and choice in everyday life?

_____
_____
_____
_____
_____

And finally as I shared in 9.2 in *Wholehearted*:

> *Transition periods are frustrating at times. We might feel stretched and it is not always about being calm. But as a result, we find ourselves connected to the earth, to practical issues, to our more spiritual self. Much as the ocean invites us to connect at a deeper level just by its presence or the sound of the waves coming into the shore, transition invites us home. A homecoming can be in many guises. What is yours?*

From reading *Wholehearted* and working through this *Wholehearted Companion Workbook,* how has transition invited you home?

THANK YOU

Thank you for reading *Wholehearted* and for working through the *Wholehearted Companion Workbook*. This truly shows a deep commitment to self-leadership and a positive and creative path through transition and I hope these insights help you.

Congratulations and keep journeying deep into your wholehearted stories!

I encourage you to share what you have learnt about yourself, your self-leadership, personality, creativity and transition from reading and applying these ideas to inspire others!

BIBLIOGRAPHY

Baird, J, *Phosphorescence: on awe, wonder and things that sustain you when the world goes dark*, HarperCollins, Sydney, 2020.

Bard, EM, *This is for you: a creative toolkit for better self-care*, Watkins, London, 2018.

Bennet, A, *The shadows of type: psychological type through seven levels of development*, Lulu, Morrisville, NC, 2010.

Berens, LV, *Understanding yourself and others: an introduction to interaction styles 2.0*, Telos Publications, Huntington Beach, CA, 2008.

Blair, S, *Invoking the inferior function*. https://www.bapt.org.uk/articles/invoking-the-inferior-function/

Blair, S & S Nash, *The type trilogy—personality cards and guidebook*, Personality Dynamics Ltd and Em-Power UK Ltd, NZ/UK, 2013.

Bridges, S, *Bridges transition model*. https://wmbridges.com/about/what-is-transition/

Campbell, J, *The hero with a thousand faces*, New World Library, Novato, CA, 2008. (First published 1949.)

Cameron, J, *The artist's way: a spiritual path to higher creativity*, Tarcher, New York, 1992.

Cohen, S, *Fierce on the page: become the writer you were meant to be and succeed on your own terms*, Writer's Digest Books, Cincinnati, OH, 2016.

Crispin, J, *The creative tarot: a modern guide to an inspired life*, Touchstone, New York, 2016.

Enz, K & J Talarico, 'Forks in the road: memories of turning points and transitions', *Applied Cognitive Psychology*, vol. 30, no. 2, 2016, pp. 188–95.

Fradera, A, 'Your life story is made up of transitions and turning points: do you know the difference?', *Research Digest*, 2015. https://digest.bps.org.uk/2015/12/10/your-life-story-is-made-up-of-transitions-and-turning-points-do-you-know-the-difference/

Gilbert, E, *Big magic: creative living beyond fear*, Bloomsbury, London, 2015.

Gilkey, C, *How to be a productive powerhouse using time blocking.* https://www.productiveflourishing.com/time-blocking/

Gruel, N, *The power of NOTEs: how non-ordinary transcendent experiences transform the way we live, love and lead,* Black Card Books, Stouffville, ON, 2018.

Hendricks, G, *The big leap: conquer your hidden fear and take life to the next level,* HarperOne, New York, 2010.

Jarvis, P, *Company of one: why staying small is the next big thing for business,* Penguin, London, 2020.

Johnston, JG, *Jung's indispensable compass: navigating the dynamics of personality types,* MSE Press, USA, 2016.

Jung, CG, 'A psychological theory of types', in *Modern man in search of a soul,* Routledge & Kegan Paul, London, 1933.

Jung, CG, 'Psychological types', *Collected works of CG Jung,* Volume 6, Bollingen Series XX, Princeton University Press, NJ, 1990.

Keirsey, D, *Please understand me II,* Prometheus Nemesis Book Company, Del Mar, CA, 1998.

Kethledge, RM & MS Erwin, *Lead yourself first: inspiring leadership through solitude,* Bloomsbury, New York, 2017.

LaPorte, D, *The desire map: a guide to what you want the most,* White Hot Press & Danielle LaPorte Inc., Canada, 2012.

LaPorte, D, *White hot truth: clarity for keeping it real on your spiritual path from one seeker to another,* Virtuonica, Vancouver, BC, 2017.

McCarthy, C & D LaPorte, *Style Statement: live by your own design,* Little, Brown & Co., New York, 2008.

McGuiness, M, *You've got personality,* MaryMac Books, Sydney, 2004.

Moody, R, M Majors & M Barimany, *What's new in type? (1/3).* https://www.bapt.org.uk/articles/whats-new-in-type-pt-1/

Nardi, D, *8 keys to self-leadership: from awareness to action,* Telos Publications, Huntington Beach, CA, 2005.

Nardi, D, *Neuroscience of personality: brain savvy insights for all types of people,* Radiance House, Los Angeles, CA, 2011.

Parker, J, *Priestess: ancient spiritual wisdom for modern sacred women,* Kind Press, Newcastle, NSW, 2020.

Pink, DH, *When: the scientific secrets of perfect timing*, Riverhead Books, New York, 2018.

Popova, M, *Networked knowledge and combinatorial creativity*, 2011. https://www.brainpickings.org/2011/08/01/networked-knowledge-combinatorial-creativity/

Pressfield, S, *The war of art: break through the blocks and win your inner creative battles*, Rugged Land, New York, 2002.

Pressfield, S, *Turning pro: tap your inner power and create your life's work*, Black Irish Books, New York, 2012.

Quenk, NL, *In the grip: understanding type, stress and the inferior function*, CPP Inc., Mountain View, CA, 2000.

Rainer, T, *The new diary: how to use a journal for self-guidance and expanded creativity*, Angus & Robertson, Sydney, 1978.

Slim, P, *Body of work: finding the thread that ties your story together*, Penguin, New York, 2013.

Spencer, E, *Lunar abundance: cultivating joy, peace and purpose using the phases of the moon*, Hachette/Running Press, Philadelphia, 2018.

Stothart, C, *How to get on with anyone*, Pearson, Harlow, UK, 2018.

Torkildson, MM, *The inner tree: discovering the roots of your intuition and overcoming barriers to mastering it*, Citrine, Asheville, NC, 2018.

Vogler, C, *The writer's journey: mythic structure for writers*, 3rd edn, Michael Wiese Productions, Studio City, CA, 2007.

Whyte, D, *Crossing the unknown sea: work as a pilgrimage of identity*, Riverhead Books, New York, 2001.

QUIET WRITING BLOG POSTS, ARTICLES AND GUEST POSTS

Bell, K, *Our heart always knows the way—a wholehearted story*, 2017. https://www.quietwriting.com/heart-way-wholehearted-story/

Connellan, T, *How to read for more creativity, pleasure and productivity,* 2017. https://www.quietwriting.com/read-creativity-pleasure-productivity/

Connellan, T, *Introverted and extraverted intuition—how to make intuition a strong practice,* 2017. https://www.quietwriting.com/introverted-extraverted-intuition/

Connellan, T, *Personality, story and introverted intuition,* 2017. https://www.quietwriting.com/personality-story-introverted-intuition/

Connellan, T, *Reading as creative influence—36 books that shaped my story,* 2017. https://www.quietwriting.com/reading-creative-influence/

Connellan, T, *Shining a quiet life: working the gifts of introversion,* 2017. https://www.quietwriting.com/shining-quiet-light-introversion/

Connellan, T, *20 practical ways of showing up and being brave (and helpful),* 2017. https://www.quietwriting.com/20-practical-ways-showing-up/

Connellan, T, *Sacred Creative Collective Group Coaching, 2021.* https://www.quietwriting.com/ sacred-creative/

Connellan, T, *Self-leadership as the most authentic heart of leadership,* 2021. https://www.quietwriting.com/self-leadership-authentic-heart-leadership/

Connellan, T, *Personality Stories Coaching.* https://www.quietwriting. com/personality-stories-coaching

Connellan, T, *Stories of wholehearted living.* https://www.quietwriting. com/stories-of-wholehearted-living/

Hanford-Day, L, *From breakdown to breakthrough: my wholehearted life,* 2018. https://www.quietwriting.com/ breakdown-to-breakthrough/

Herriman, J, *Embracing a creative life—a wholehearted story,* 2017. https://www.quietwriting.com/embracing-creative-life/

Love, P, *The journey to write here—my wholehearted story*, 2018. https://www.quietwriting.com/journey-to-write-here/

Morgan, S. *Writing the way through—a wholehearted story*, 2019. https://www.quietwriting.com/writing-the-way-through/

Pilz, K, *Grief and pain can be our most important teachers—a wholehearted story*, 2018. https://www.quietwriting.com/grief-and-pain/

Washburn, H, *When the inner voice calls, and calls, again—my journey to wholehearted living,* 2018. https://www.quietwriting.com/inner-voice/

TAROT AND ORACLE DECKS AND GUIDEBOOKS

Baron-Reid, C, *The enchanted map—oracle cards and guidebook*, Hay House, Carlsbad, CA, 2011.

Baron-Reid, C, *The wisdom of the oracle—card deck and guidebook*, Hay House, Carlsbad, CA, 2015.

Crispin, J & J May, *The spolia tarot—deck and guidebook*, 2018.

Evans, ME, *Vessel oracle deck*, 2016.

Fairchild, A, *Sacred rebels oracle*, Blue Angels Publishing, Melbourne, 2014.

Krans, K, *The wild unknown animal—spirit deck and guidebook*, Wild Unknown, 2016.

Kroll, M, *Sacred symbols for divination and meditation—oracle deck and guidebook*, Marcella Kroll, 2013–2015.

Livingstone, C, *The art of life tarot*, US Games Systems, 2012.

Sakki, MC, *The Sakki Sakki tarot & guidebook*, MPress, 2004.

ABOUT THE AUTHOR

Terri Connellan is a certified life coach, writer and accredited psychological type practitioner. She has a Master of Arts in Language and Literacy, two teaching qualifications and a successful 30-year career as a teacher and a leader in adult vocational education. Her coaching and writing focus on three elements—creativity, personality and self-leadership—especially for women in transition to a life with deeper purpose. Terri works with women globally through her creative business, Quiet Writing, encouraging deeper self-understanding of body of work, creativity and psychological type for more wholehearted and fulfilling lives. She lives and writes in a village on the outskirts of Sydney surrounded by beach and bush.

CONNECTING AND SHARING

Thank you for reading *Wholehearted: Self-leadership for women in transition* and this *Wholehearted Companion Workbook*. Please share the learning and experiences forward and help other readers to find this book and workbook. Here are some suggestions for you:

- Write an online review or blog about *Wholehearted* to help people realise its benefits.
- Gift this book to family, clients and friends.
- Share on social media with any photos of you reading *Wholehearted* with the tags #wholeheartedbook #selfleadershipbook #TerriConnellan
- Invite Terri to speak with your association or club, including virtually.
- Discuss *Wholehearted* at your book club. Work with the Book Club notes at QuietWriting.com/WholeheartedBookClubNotes.
- Connect with Terri by visiting QuietWriting.com or on social media where she is @writingquietly

ENDNOTES

1. D Whyte, *Crossing the unknown sea: work as a pilgrimage of identity*, Riverhead Books, New York, 2001.

2. J Campbell, *The hero with a thousand faces*, New World Library, California, 2008 (first published 1949).

3. C Vogler, *The writer's journey: mythic structure for writers*, 3rd edn, Michael Wiese Productions, Studio City, CA, 2007, p. 87.

4. K Enz & J Talarico, 'Forks in the road: memories of turning points and transitions', *Applied Cognitive Psychology*, vol. 30, no. 2, 2016, pp. 188–95.

5. A Fradera, 'Your life story is made up of transitions and turning points: do you know the difference?', *Research Digest*, 2015. https://digest.bps.org.uk/2015/12/10/your-life-story-is-made-up-of-transitions-and-turning-points-do-you-know-the-difference/

6. S Bridges, *Bridges transition model*. https://wmbridges.com/about/what-is-transition/

7. T Connellan, *20 practical ways of showing up and being brave (and helpful)*—Quiet Writing, 2017. https://www.quietwriting.com/20-practical-ways-showing-up/

8. E Bard, *This is for you: A creative toolkit for better self-care*, Watkins, London, 2018.

9. Beautiful You Coaching Academy. https://www.beautifulyoucoachingacademy.com/

10. T Connellan, *Shining a quiet light: working the gifts of introversion*—Quiet Writing, 2017. https://www.quietwriting.com/shining-quiet-light-introversion/

11. T Connellan, *Personality, story and introverted intuition*—Quiet Writing, 2017. https://www.quietwriting.com/personality-story-introverted-intuition/

12. S King, *Danse Macabre*, Simon and Schuster, New York, 2011, p. 88.

13. T Connellan, *How to read for more creativity, pleasure and productivity*—Quiet Writing, 2017. https://www.quietwriting.com/read-creativity-pleasure-productivity/

14. T Connellan, *Stories of wholehearted living*—Quiet Writing. https://www.quietwriting.com/stories-of-wholehearted-living/

15   T Connellan, *Self-leadership as the most authentic heart of leadership*—Quiet Writing, 2021. https://www.quietwriting.com/self-leadership-authentic-heart-leadership/
16   J Penn *How to get a book published: traditional, self-publishing, print-on-demand, ebooks and audiobooks.* https://www.thecreativepenn.com/publishing/
17   A Adrian. https://www.amberadrian.com/
18   K Pilz, *Why luck had nothing to do with my self-directed life.* https://www.writeyourjourney.com/a-self-directed-life-is-not-luck/
19   S Holmes, http://www.sharynholmes.com/
20   G Hendricks, *The big leap: conquer your hidden fear and take life to the next level*, HarperOne, New York, 2010.
21   T Connellan, *Reading as creative influence—36 books that shaped my story*, 2017. https://www.quietwriting.com/reading-creative-influence/
22   J Penn, 'Writing the darkness and tips for audiodrama, with AK Benedict', *The creative penn podcast.* https://www.thecreativepenn.com/2017/10/30/writing-darkness-audio-drama-ak-benedict/
23   About Joanna Penn. https://www.thecreativepenn.com/about/
24   T Connellan, *Sacred Creative Collective Group Coaching*—Quiet Writing, 2021. https:// www.quietwriting.com/sacred-creative/
25   S Pressfield, *Turning pro: tap your inner power and create your life's work*, Black Irish Books, New York, 2012, p. 13.
26   T Connellan, *Reading as creative influence.* https://www.quietwriting.com/reading-creative-influence/
27   T Rainer, *The new diary: how to use a journal for self-guidance and expanded creativity*, Angus & Robertson, Sydney, 1978.
28   CG Jung, A psychological theory of types, in *Modern man in search of a soul*, Routledge & Kegan Paul, London, 1933, pp. 107–8.
29   M McGuiness, *You've got personality*, MaryMac Books, Sydney, 2004, p. 3.
30   CG Jung, Psychological types, *Collected works of CG Jung*, vol. 6, Bollingen Series XX, Princeton University Press, NJ, 1990. (Originally published in German in 1921.)
31   M McGuiness, *You've got personality*, pp. 6–7.
32   D Nardi, *Neuroscience of personality: brain savvy insights for all types of people*, Radiance House, Los Angeles, CA, 2011.

33 D Nardi, *8 keys to self-leadership: from awareness to action*, Telos Publications, Huntington Beach, CA, 2005.

34 D Keirsey, *Please understand me II*, Prometheus Nemesis Book Company, Del Mar, CA, 1998.

35 C Stothart, *How to get on with anyone*, Pearson, Harlow, UK, 2018.

36 LV Berens, *Understanding yourself and others: an introduction to interaction styles 2.0*, Telos Publications, Huntington Beach, CA, 2008.

37 T Connellan, *Personality Stories Coaching*—Quiet Writing. https://www.quietwriting.com/personality-stories-coaching/

38 RM Kethledge & MS Erwin, *Lead yourself first: inspiring leadership through solitude*, Bloomsbury, New York, 2017.

39 Sacred Creative Pinterest board. https://www.pinterest.com.au/writingquietly/sacred-creative/

40 *16 style types.* https://16styletypes.com/

41 C McCarthy & D LaPorte, *Style Statement: live by your own design*, Little, Brown & Co., New York, 2008.

42 D LaPorte, *The desire map: a guide to what you want the most*, White Hot Press & Danielle LaPorte Inc., Canada, 2012.

43 T Connellan, *Welcome to Quiet Writing*—Quiet Writing, 2016. https://www.quietwriting.com/welcome-to-quiet-writing/

44 P Slim, *Body of work: finding the thread that ties your story together*, Penguin, New York, 2013. p. 7.

45 K Enz & J Talarico, 'Forks in the road: memories of turning points and transitions', *Applied Cognitive Psychology*, vol. 30, no. 2, 2016, pp. 188–95.

46 L Hanford-Day, *Breakdown to breakthrough: my wholehearted life*—Quiet Writing, 2018. https://www.quietwriting.com/breakdown-to-breakthrough/

47 H Washburn, *When the inner voice calls, and calls, again—my journey to wholehearted living*—Quiet Writing, 2018. https://www.quietwriting.com/inner-voice/

48 K Bell, *Our heart always knows the way: a wholehearted story*—Quiet Writing, 2017. https://www.quietwriting.com/heart-way-wholehearted-story/

49 J Crispin, *The creative tarot: a modern guide to an inspired life*, Touchstone, New York, 2016, p. 195.

50 E Spencer, *Lunar abundance: cultivating joy, peace and purpose using the phases of the moon*, Hachette/Running Press, Philadelphia, 2018.

51 J Penn, 'Self-care and productivity for authors with Ellen Bard', *The creative penn podcast*. https://www.thecreativepenn.com/2016/08/01/self-care-productivity-ellen-bard/

52 P Love, *The journey to write here —my wholehearted story* —Quiet Writing, 2018. https://www.quietwriting.com/journey-to-write-here/

53 T Connellan, *NaNoWriMo: 10 lessons on the value of writing each day* —Quiet Writing, 2017. https://www.quietwriting.com/nanowrimo-10-lessons-writing-each-day/

54 J Baird, *Phosphorescence: on awe, wonder and things that sustain you when the world goes dark*, HarperCollins Publishers, Sydney, Kindle edn, 2020, p. 23.

55 T Connellan, *10 amazing life lessons from swimming in the sea*—Quiet Writing, 2017. https://www.quietwriting.com/10-life-lessons-swimming-sea/

56 RM Kethledge & MS Erwin, *Lead yourself first: inspiring leadership through solitude*, Bloomsbury, New York, 2017.

57 Kethledge & Erwin, *Lead yourself first: inspiring leadership through solitude*.

58 M McGuiness, *You've got personality*, Mary Mac Books, Sydney, 2004. pp. 6–7.

59 JG Johnston, *Jung's indispensable compass: navigating the dynamics of personality types*, MSE Press, USA, 2016.

60 N Gruel, *The power of NOTEs: how non-ordinary transcendent experiences transform the way we live, love and lead*, Black Card Books, Stouffville, ON, 2018, pp. 40–5.

61 S Blair & S Nash, *The type trilogy—card sets for 3 type lenses and complete guidebook,* Personality Dynamics Ltd and Em-Power UK Ltd, NZ/UK, 2013.

62 D Keirsey, *Please understand me II,* Prometheus Nemesis Book Co., California, 1998.

63 T Connellan, *Personality Stories Coaching.* https://www.quietwriting.com/personality-stories-coaching

64 C Gilkey, *How to be a productive powerhouse using time blocking.* https://www.productiveflourishing.com/time-blocking/

65 EL Doctorow interview (1986), *The art of fiction*, no. 94, *Paris Review*, issue 101. https://www.theparisreview.org/interviews/2718/the-art-of-fiction-no-94-e-l-doctorow

66 N Newman with H Carr, *The art of creative living podcast: creating a business in line with your values.* https://www.nicolanewman.com/creating-business-values-hayley-carr/

67 P Jarvis, *Company of one: why staying small is the next big thing for business,* Penguin, UK, 2020.

68 T Connellan, *Sacred creative collective.* https://www.quietwriting.com/sacred-creative/

69 Susannah Conway on Instagram. https://www.instagram.com/susannahconway/

70 DH Pink, *When: the scientific secrets of perfect timing,* Riverhead Books, New York, 2018.

71 J Carrington, *Living and working in seasons.* http://www.jencarrington.com/make-it-happen-a-podcast-for-bloggers-and-creatives/2017/5/16/living-and-working-in-seasons

72 J Parker, *Priestess: ancient spiritual wisdom for modern sacred women,* Kind Press, Newcastle, NSW, 2020.

73 D Nardi, *Neuroscience of personality: brain savvy insights for all types of people,* Radiance House, Los Angeles, CA, 2011, p. 103.

74 T Connellan, *Introverted and extraverted intuition—how to make intuition a strong practice —Quiet Writing, 2017.* https://www.quietwriting.com/introverted-extraverted-intuition/

75 MM Torkildson, *The inner tree: discovering the roots of your intuition and overcoming barriers to mastering it,* Citrine, Asheville, NC, 2018.

76 Cerries Mooney. https://cerriesmooney.com/

77 T Connellan, *Reading as creative influence.* https://www.quietwriting.com/reading-creative-influence/

78 M Popova, *Networked knowledge and combinatorial creativity,* 2011. https://www.brainpickings.org/2011/08/01/networked-knowledge-combinatorial-creativity/

79 T Connellan, *Reading as creative influence.* https://www.quietwriting.com/reading-creative-influence/

80 M Popova, *Networked knowledge and combinatorial creativity,* 2011.

81 S Cohen, *Fierce on the page: become the writer you were meant to be and succeed on your own terms,* Writer's Digest Books, Cincinnati, OH, 2016, pp. 56–7.

82 S Pressfield, *The war of art: break through the blocks and win your inner creative battles,* Rugged Land, New York, 2002, p. 165.

83 Saboteur Questionnaire. https://www.positiveintelligence.com/assessments/

84 L Hanford-Day, *From breakdown to breakthrough: my wholehearted life*. https://www.quietwriting.com/breakdown-to-breakthrough/

85 K Pilz, *Grief and pain can be our most important teachers—a wholehearted story*—Quiet Writing, 2018. https://www.quietwriting.com/grief-and-pain/

86 J Herriman, *Embracing a creative life—a wholehearted story* —Quiet Writing, 2017. https://www.quietwriting.com/embracing-creative-life/

87 S Morgan, *Writing the way through—a wholehearted story* —Quiet Writing, 2019. https://www.quietwriting.com/writing-the-way-through/

88 A Bennet, *The shadows of type: psychological type through seven levels of development*, Lulu, Morrisville, NC, 2010, p. 43.

89 R Moody, M Majors & M Barimany, *What's new in type? (1/3)*. https://www.bapt.org.uk/articles/whats-new-in-type-pt-1/

90 D Nardi, *8 keys to self-leadership: from awareness to action*, Telos Publications, Huntington Beach, CA, 2005, p. 22.

91 A Bennet, *The shadows of type: psychological type through seven levels of development*, Lulu, Morrisville, NC, 2010, pp. 17–19.

92 NL Quenk, *In the grip: understanding type, stress and the inferior function*, CPP Inc., Mountain View, CA, 2000.

93 M McGuiness, *You've got personality*, Mary Mac Books, Sydney, 2004, p. 35.

94 S Blair, *Invoking the inferior function*, https://www.bapt.org.uk/articles/invoking-the-inferior-function/

95 T Connellan *Personality Stories Coaching*. https://www.quietwriting.com/personality-stories-coaching/

96 E Gilbert, *Big magic: creative living beyond fear*, Bloomsbury, London, 2015, pp. 42–57.

97 J Cameron, *The artist's way: a spiritual path to higher creativity*, Tarcher, New York, 1992, pp. 123–4.

Myers–Briggs Type Indicator, Myers Briggs and MBTI are trademarks or registered trademarks of The Myers & Briggs Foundation in the United States and other countries.

CPSIA information can be obtained
at www.ICGtesting.com
Printed in the USA
LVHW030119170821
695429LV00005B/184